W9-BLY-489

Mexican Americans and the Question of Race

Mexican Americans and the Question of Race

JULIE A. DOWLING

University of Texas Press ⬥ *Austin*

Copyright © 2014 by the University of Texas Press
All rights reserved

First paperback edition, 2015

Requests for permission to reproduce material from this work should be sent to:
  Permissions
  University of Texas Press
  P.O. Box 7819
  Austin, TX 78713–7819
  http://utpress.utexas.edu/index.php/rp-form

♾ The paper used in this book meets the minimum requirements of ANSI/NISO
Z39.48–1992 (R1997) (Permanence of Paper).

Library of Congress Cataloging-in-Publication Data
Dowling, Julie A., 1975–
  Mexican Americans and the question of race / Julie A. Dowling. — First edition.
    pages   cm
  Includes bibliographical references and index.
  ISBN 978-0-292-75401-0 (cloth : alk. paper)
  ISBN 978-1-4773-0754-0 (paperback)
1. Mexican Americans—Race identity.   2. United States—Race relations.
3. Mexican Americans—Social conditions.   I. Title.
  E184.M5D69   2014
  305.868′72073—dc23

                                                                    2013024218

doi:10.7560/754010

Contents

Acknowledgments

There are many individuals whom I would like to thank for their assistance in the lengthy journey toward the completion of this book. First, this project began during my graduate studies at the University of Texas at Austin (UT), and I would like to thank the faculty, graduate students, and staff of the Department of Sociology, the Center for Mexican American Studies, and the Population Research Center there for funding and other intangible support I received over the years from each of these communities. While conducting the early stages of this research, I was also funded by the National Science Foundation (NSF) through an NSF Minority Graduate Fellowship and an NSF Dissertation Improvement Grant.

Several current and former faculty at UT provided feedback that shaped the direction of this study, including Chris Ellison, Bob Hummer, Craig Watkins, Maya Charrad, Martha Menchaca, Neil Foley, Susan González Baker, and Gloria González-López. Both Chris Ellison and Susan González Baker have seen the project through as it evolved substantially from a simple exploration of variables that shape the labeling of Mexican Americans and Mexican immigrants to a book that explores the crucial role of racial ideology in labeling practices for these populations. Without their support and guidance, I would never have been able to see this through.

Other friends who were pillars of support during my time in Austin and beyond include Alison Newby, Danny Cortese, Mari Infante, Ana Saldaña-Thyagaraja, Rebecca Skinner, Rebekah Nix Granbery, Jacob Steelman, David Olson, Maria Lowe, Brian Williams, Ramon Rivera-Servera, Mary Beltrán, Joby Dixon, John Morán González, Isabela Quintana, Laura Padilla, Marilyn Espitia, Betsy Guzmán, Jenifer Bratter, Greg Carter, and Chiyuma Elliott. Alison Newby, my dear friend and collaborator on numerous other projects, and whom I affectionately refer to as "the other half of my brain," has been especially supportive over the past fifteen years since our time as officemates at UT. Danny Cortese, one of the brightest and most hilarious people I have ever known, also occupies a special place in my heart, as we have continually traveled side by side through each hurdle of academic life. Thank you, Danny, for always making me laugh through the painful parts of this process.

Before making the transition to my job at the University of Illinois at Urbana-Champaign, I spent a year in the Department of Sociology at the University of California at Santa Barbara as a UC President's Postdoctoral Fellow. I would like to thank the postdoctoral program, the Sociology Department, and my faculty mentor and friend Denise Segura for this wonderful opportunity. Conversations with members of the faculty at UCSB most definitely helped to shape the direction of the project.

In the Department of Latina/Latino Studies at the University of Illinois, I have been blessed with amazing colleagues who have offered their support and guidance. I would like to thank the staff, Alicia Rodriguez and Laura Castañeda, and our faculty and affiliates: Ricky Rodríguez, Lisa Cacho, Edna Viruell-Fuentes, Isabel Molina-Guzmán, Alejandro Lugo, Gilberto Rosas, Rolando Romero, Mireya Loza, Jorge Chapa, Adrian Burgos, and Dara Goldman. In particular, Ricky was incredibly encouraging of my project from the outset. Additionally, I owe a special debt of gratitude to Lisa and Alejandro, who read drafts of some of the chapters, providing important feedback.

Outside Illinois, a number of colleagues shared their publishing insights that proved incredibly helpful. For this advice, I would like to thank Zulema Valdez, Tyrone Foreman, Wendy Roth, Victor Rios, Tomás Jiménez, Jessica Vasquez, Tanya Golash-Boza, and Cecilia Menjívar. I will forever be indebted to Cecilia for connecting me with Theresa May at the University of Texas Press. I would like to thank Theresa for her enthusiasm and support of my project from the beginning. Moreover, I would also like to thank Sandra Spicher and Nancy Moore for their help throughout the copyediting phase of production. The book was also shaped by the editorial skills of Karen Ivy, who helped with both organizational work and copyediting on portions of the manuscript. Moreover, comments from Edward Murguía and an anonymous reviewer were incredibly helpful and I believe made this a much stronger book.

As I was completing the final edits for the book, I was invited to participate in a two-part workshop on the U.S. Census Alternative Questionnaire Experiment (AQE) that was convened in Washington, DC, and then at the Population Association (PAA) meetings. Our stimulating dialogues at both events re-energized me and allowed me to forge through the final editing stages. I would like to thank Linda Gage at PAA for organizing these events, as well as Nicholas Jones, Roberto Ramírez, and Joan Hill at the U.S. Census Bureau. I would also like to thank the other participants: Ann Morning, Aliya Saperstein, John Iceland, Jennifer Lee, Ken Prewitt, Matthew Snipp, and Carolyn Liebler.

On a personal note, I would like to thank a number of people here in Champaign-Urbana who provided emotional support during this journey. Rachel Gonsalves, Lori Cuffey, Karen Street, and I have seen each other through a rollercoaster of life events this past seven years. I am thankful every day that I met the three of you. I would also like to thank all the members of my "Ladies Night Out" crew, especially Margaret Kelley, Gayle Magee, and Beth Robischon for making me laugh until my sides hurt, even in the midst of all my stress. I would like to thank Belinda De La Rosa and Jorge Chapa for many outstanding meals at "La Casa Chapa-Rosa" and for all their support over the years.

Additionally, some truly amazing graduate students at Illinois have inspired me throughout my writing process with the energy they bring to the classroom including especially Myrian Luis, Mariana Martinez, Blanca Rincon, Joanna Perez, and Eduardo Coronel. I owe a special thanks to Joanna, who always seemed to sense when I was feeling stuck in my writing process and would send me an encouraging note at just the right moment. It has been a pleasure working with these and so many other graduate and undergraduate students here.

Most importantly, I would like to thank my family, including my mother Marie, my father Jim, and my brother Joe and his wife Linda, for their support over the years. My mother and my *tias* Katie, Liz, Lilia, Norma, and Daisy were all instrumental in conducting the research for this book by helping me to establish connections in each of my field sites. This was truly a family effort, and they share in my accomplishments. I would also like to thank the interviewees who shared their time and stories with me. This book would never have been possible without their generosity and hospitality.

Finally, my husband Jonathan Xavier Inda and our beautiful four-year-old daughter Sofia brighten my days with more joy than I could have ever imagined. I am thankful to have such a wonderful family to come home to, and especially grateful for all the help Jonathan has provided in doing more than his fair share of child care and other household responsibilities during my completion of this book. And, for my daughter, who recently asked with exasperation, "Is Mommy's book done yet?" . . . Yes, *mija*, it is.

Mexican Americans and the Question of Race

CHAPTER 1

The Question of Race

Miguel Gonzalez grew up in an impoverished *colonia* on the outskirts of Mission, just across the border from Mexico in the Rio Grande Valley of South Texas.[1] As a child, Miguel worked the fields with his family, migrating seasonally to pick crops in other states. He vividly recalls the discrimination they faced, including once being asked to leave a restaurant that was for "whites only." He said, "A lot of people, they wouldn't like us because we were migrants. . . . Back then it was like if you don't have this or that, then you're nobody." At forty-five years old, Miguel still lives in Mission and now works as a janitor. He has a dark-brown complexion and says there is no question that when others see him, they see a "Mexican." In fact, he is often mistaken for an immigrant. Yet, despite Miguel's experiences with being classified and treated as nonwhite, he selected "white" for his race on the U.S. Census form, explaining, "'cause I'm an American, right?" His question belies ambivalence about whether this identity really belongs to him. Miguel admitted he could not think of any situation outside the context of the census where he would use the word "white" to describe himself. His formal assertion of whiteness expresses a desire to be seen as fully American.

Like Miguel, Eduardo "Eddie" Martinez spent his childhood working alongside his family in the fields. His great-grandparents migrated to Texas from northern Mexico, and he was born and raised in the barrio of San Felipe in Del Rio, Texas, located on the Mexican border directly west of San Antonio. After college, Eddie returned to teach in his hometown. During the course of his subsequent career as an educator, he witnessed a great deal of change, including the 1971 court-mandated consolidation of Del Rio's separate Anglo[2] and Mexican school districts. Decades earlier, Del Rio was the location of the first-ever school desegregation case involving Mexican Americans. In 1930, Mexican American parents went to court to argue that because Mexicans were racially white, they should not be segregated from Anglo students. Their efforts reflected a common strategy of this time period that relied on public articulations of whiteness to combat segregation. The court did rule that Mexicans could not be "arbitrarily segregated" from "other white races," but it was not a victory for Del Rio's Mexican American community because the district was still allowed to continue segregation based on alleged linguistic and cultural needs (Foley 2006). While the case took place before Eddie was born, its legacy informs his racial identification today. Eddie checked "white" for his race, citing the court decision. Yet, like Miguel, Eddie would never describe himself as "white" in any other setting. When discussing his choice, he said, "That doesn't change who I am. I'm still a Mexican."

Juliana Sanchez, a retired teacher's assistant in Fort Worth, Texas, is also the child of migrant workers. Her father was born in Mexico, and her mother was third-generation Mexican American. She remembers attending separate "Mexican" schools and "knowing there were many places Mexicans were not allowed to go." But her approach to the census race question was different from that of Miguel and Eddie. While Juliana's skin color is the lightest of the three, she says she would never identify as white in any context. That is simply not how she sees herself, nor how others have classified her. Instead, Juliana marked "other race" and wrote, "Mexican," explaining, "I'm very proud of my race."

Juliana grew up in a working-class neighborhood with a mixture of Mexicans and African Americans who lived "all poor, all together." She credits African Americans with "helping to open a lot of doors" for Mexican Americans, and she comments on the similarities between these two "racial" groups. Juliana worked in bilingual education for many years and also feels strongly about the plight of undocumented immigrants. Thus, she is often frustrated with Mexican Americans who discriminate against both African Americans and Mexican immigrants, explaining, "Our situation is just like the blacks, like them we have struggled against discrimination. We should work with them and with immigrants, all of us together." Juliana chose to self-identify as "Mexican" on the census, both expressing her solidarity with Mexican immigrants and defining Mexican Americans as a "racial" group in the United States.

I present the stories of Miguel, Eddie, and Juliana here precisely because they share so many similarities. All three are children of migrant workers, experienced economic hardships, and endured overt forms of racial discrimination. All three speak Spanish and English fluently, currently live in majority-Mexican neighborhoods, have primarily Mexican-origin friends, and married Mexican Americans. Yet despite their commonalities, they each approach the question of race differently. What is it that leads to their divergent racial responses? It is easy to understand how Juliana's strong attachment to her culture, association with African Americans, and her experiences with racial discrimination would steer her to identify as racially "other," but why do Miguel and Eddie select a racial category that does not resonate with their experiences? Moreover, as neither of these men would identify as white outside the census context, how does their racial self-identification vary based on audience? In what settings do Mexican Americans use labels such as "white," "Hispanic," "Mexican," or "Mexican American," and what are the meanings they attach to these terms? Moreover, what do the uses of these labels reveal about the racial experiences of Mexican Americans? *Mexican Americans and the Question of Race* is an exploration of what shapes racial labeling practices for Mexican Americans and Mexican immigrants, with particular attention to the disconnect between public and private articulations of race and the role of racial ideology in the process of racial identification.

The Racial Place of Latinos

With the increasing presence of Latinos in the United States, the demographics of the country's future will be shaped in large part by the assimilation and racial identification patterns of this group. Indeed, according to the 2010 Census, Latinos now constitute 16% of the U.S. population and account for over half of the nation's growth over the past ten years.[3] Much of this reflects an expanding Mexican-origin population, as nearly two-thirds of all Latinos in the United States are of Mexican ancestry (Ennis et al. 2011). Perspectives on the racial identification and assimilation trajectory of Latinos have been and continue to be a constant source of debate. Indeed, the media tend to portray the growing Latino population as a threat to the economic and cultural fabric of the nation (Chavez 2008). Much of this scrutiny is based on the assumption that Latinos fracture American society by maintaining identities that counter the dominant Anglo culture (Huntington 2004; Buchanan 2007). Among scholars there is considerable disagreement regarding these issues, but while perspectives on the assimilation patterns of Latinos vary considerably, there are three main arguments.

First, some scholars believe that Latinos are not assimilating into the dominant white majority, either by choice or as a result of exclusion. At one extreme of this perspective, political scientist Samuel Huntington argues that Mexican Americans and other Latinos refuse to learn English and acclimate to U.S. society, a choice he says threatens to wreak havoc on the nation, both culturally and financially (Huntington 2004). Numerous studies, however, show that Latino English-language acquisition rates are in fact comparable to those of earlier waves of European immigrants (Alba 2006; Citrin et al. 2007). Moreover, scholars further challenge Huntington's hypothesis of voluntary refusal, pointing out that experiences with racial discrimination from the majority group foster and maintain racial and ethnic boundaries. Thus, continued discrimination against Latinos may counter desired integration (Telles and Ortiz 2008).

A second position regarding the assimilation trajectory of Latinos is that both individual and group characteristics may lead some Latinos to be accepted as white, while others remain racialized as nonwhite. The result is a multi-tiered racial system in which some Latinos are classified as white, others as black, and still others as somewhere in between (Bonilla-Silva 2004; Golash-Boza 2006; Golash-Boza and Darity 2008; Frank et al. 2010). Golash-Boza and Darity (2008) suggest that individual Latinos may adopt identities as white, Latino, or black based on skin color and experiences with discrimination. Bonilla-Silva (2004) posits a trichotomous racial classification system in which, based on skin color and socioeconomic status, some Latino groups may become accepted as "white" and others as "honorary whites," while the majority will become a part of the "collective black" alongside African Americans.

The third argument posits that most Latinos are following in the footsteps of European immigrants on the path toward full assimilation into the white majority (Patterson 2001; Yancey 2003; Lee and Bean 2004). Specifically, Yancey (2003) cites the significant proportion of Latinos who identify as "white" on the census as evidence that they are currently accepted as white. Moreover, drawing on a quantitative analysis of survey data, he argues that both Latinos and Asian Americans more closely resemble European Americans than they do African Americans in some key racial attitudes. In particular, he notes that Latinos "are even less supportive of talking about race than European Americans." He argues that this is indicative of their adoption of "color-blind" racial ideology, an ideological framework that involves the deliberate nonrecognition of race and racial privilege. For Yancey, this is yet another indicator that Latinos are becoming racially white. Speaking of both Latinos and Asian Americans, he writes (2003: 117), ". . . minority identity is breaking down as these nonblack minorities begin to accept the social attitudes that reflect the values of color blindness and individualism—hallmarks of a white racial identity."

But, do Latinos identify as "white" and eschew conversations about race for the same reasons as European Americans? And are Latinos who claim whiteness indeed accepted as racially white by others? Until now there has been very little qualitative investigation into the meanings Latinos themselves ascribe to formal assertions of whiteness. Sociological research in this area often draws on quantitative analysis of national surveys, specifically focusing on the degree to which Latinos identify as white on either the census or questionnaires using similar racial and ethnic options (Patterson 2001; Yancey 2003; Tafoya 2004; Frank et al. 2010). According to the U.S. Census, Latino/Hispanic is a "panethnic" category composed of persons of Spanish-speaking origin who may be of any "race."[4] Persons are first asked to indicate whether they are of Hispanic origin[5] and are then asked to answer a question on racial identification that includes options for white, black, Native American, multiple Asian-origin groups, and an "other race" category. Like Juliana, many Latinos choose to mark "other race" and write in a Latino identifier such as Hispanic or Mexican American. However, for three decades now, approximately half of the Latino population has selected "white" for their race.

The first goal of this book is to examine exactly what these public assertions of "whiteness" and racial "otherness" on the census mean to Mexican Americans.[6] While some suggest that white identification may signify lighter skin color (Denton and Massey 1989), assimilation (Yancey 2003), or greater feelings of inclusion in U.S. society (Tafoya 2004), my findings directly counter these claims.[7] Drawing on interviews with Mexican Americans in Texas, I find that choosing whiteness vs. racial "otherness" does not typically reflect such differences in color or cultural assimilation. Most "white" Mexican Americans in the study speak Spanish, identify strongly with their cultural heritage, report incidents of discrimination, and are not lighter skinned than those who label as "other race." Moreover, like Miguel and Eddie, the overwhelming majority of "white" Mexican American respondents would never use the term "white" as a self-referent outside the context of the census form. Contradicting prevalent assumptions, I find the difference between "white" and "other race" Mexican Americans lies not in how they have been racialized but in how they interpret and express their experiences with racialization through various discursive strategies.

I develop a theoretical framework to explain this process, arguing that where respondents are situated on a *racial ideology continuum* is highly influential in determining what race they choose on the census. On one end of the continuum, mirroring the dominant discourse of American meritocracy, "white" Mexican Americans frequently employ a discursive framework that can be described as "color and power evasive"[8] (Frankenberg 1993), espousing what is commonly referred to as "color-blind racial ideology." As Yancey (2003) notes, this ideology has been found primarily in studies of European Americans who discount race as an important factor in determining life chances, often not acknowledging their own racial identities as whites and the privileges attached to whiteness (Bonilla-Silva 2001; Yancey 2003). "White" Mexican American respondents often similarly minimize or deflect the role of race in their lives. However, I argue their reasons for doing so are fundamentally different from those of European Americans in that their color-blind rhetoric and claims to whiteness operate as a defensive strategy. As targets of racism, Mexican Americans in the study are actually very aware of race, and their own stories of discrimination continually contradict the racial ideology that discounts it. Throughout my interview with Miguel, for example, he discussed multiple instances of discrimination he has faced, and yet, in line with color-blind ideology, he downplayed these experiences. Instead, Miguel adheres to a philosophy that everyone can get ahead if they work hard. His motto is: "Always think positive. Leave the past in the back . . . leave the bad aside."

On the other end of the continuum, "other race" respondents often speak more candidly about the impact of race in their lives, and some even articulate strong anti-racist ideologies or counter-frames. Juliana, for example, acknowledges racism in her own life and forges alliances with African Americans and immigrants. However, not all Mexican Americans fit neatly into the categories of explicitly "color-blind" or "anti-racist" in their views on race. The racial ideology continuum I develop helps to capture the remarks of respondents like Eddie, who oscillated during the interview between talking about his experiences in highly racialized ways (including discussions of his participation in Chicano civil rights organizations as a youth) and yet still choosing to align himself with whiteness as part of a legacy of resisting racial "othering." I argue that it is crucial to understand this phenomenon of resisting racial "othering" through a historical lens. The strategy of asserting whiteness to combat discrimination has a long history in Mexican American communities (Foley 1998; Gómez 2007), and as Eddie's comments reveal, it continues to exert influence today.[9]

Overall, I find that Mexican Americans identify as "white" on the census not because they are accepted as white or even because they see themselves as white. Rather, by reframing the borders of whiteness to include them, Mexican Americans resist racial "othering," in an effort to be accepted as fully American. Yet, despite their efforts to fit within the boundaries of whiteness, continued experiences with racial profiling and discrimination reinforce their status as racial "others." Most Mexican Americans in the study, including those who identified as white, detailed accounts of racial stereotyping and differential treatment. These findings corroborate research on the persistence of racialization in the lives of Mexican Americans (Telles and Ortiz 2008; Vasquez 2011) and challenge arguments that identification with whiteness on the census is an indication that Latinos are becoming accepted into the white majority (Yancey 2003).

A substantial proportion of the Mexican-origin population in the United States is foreign born, making the racial experiences and identities of Mexican immigrants key to the investigation of Latino identity. Hence, the second goal of the book is to examine Mexican immigrants' labeling practices and the ways in which both Mexican Americans and Mexican immigrants navigate racial and ethnic identification in their daily encounters. While there are some similarities between these groups, the process of racial identity construction for immigrants differs substantially from their U.S.-born co-ethnics, as they rely on an understanding of race derived from Mexico. The dominant racial discourse in Mexico emphasizes an understanding of Mexicans as a mestizo people composed of a melding of the Spanish with the Indian (Doremus 2001; Sue 2013).[10] Immigrants in the study typically wrote in their race (*raza*) as "Mexicano/a" or "Hispanic," either asserting their *raza* in terms of national origin or identifying with a category assigned to them in a U.S. context. A few Mexican immigrants also relied on perceived social standing in Mexico prior to arrival in the United States in their decisions to identify racially as "white" or "other race." Finally, some immigrants who have spent more time in the United States asserted racial identities in ways that resembled U.S.-born Mexican Americans, relying on experiences with racial classification in the United States, positioning themselves relative to African Americans, or doing both.

Mexican immigrants and Mexican Americans further construct their racial identities in dialogue with and often in opposition to each other. I explore how context and audience shape racial and ethnic labeling for both groups in their interactions with each other and with other racial groups. Overall, racial labeling among my respondents is shaped by multiple factors, including to whom one is speaking and in what language, and whether the goal of the interaction is to express sameness or difference. Racial ideology also influences this process of identity assertions, as it informs with whom respondents wish to align themselves in a given interaction.

Guided theoretically by an identity constructionist framework, I argue that my respondents' racial and ethnic identities are the result of an ongoing dialogue between "external" assigned identities from others and "internal" asserted identities. As a result of this dialectical process, racial identities are not fixed or static but dynamic and highly contingent (Nagel 1994; Cornell and Hartmann 1997). I integrate scholarship on Latino racial identity formation with theories of whiteness and racial ideology, including the "white racial frame" (Feagin 2010), and the concepts of "color and power evasive" (Frankenberg 1993) and "color-blind" (Bonilla-Silva 2001) racial ideologies. Drawing from these multiple perspectives, I create a conceptual model that highlights the connection between racial ideology and both public and personal articulations of race.

While most studies focus either on formal racial labeling on surveys or on ways in which respondents label themselves in daily life, *Mexican Americans and the Question of Race* provides a more comprehensive study that explores both these aspects of identification. Research on Latino racial and ethnic identification tends to focus on personal traits (physical appearance and surname), cultural attributes (Spanish language ability and cultural competency), social dimensions (friends, dating, and marriage), and encounters with racial discrimination. Rarely do such studies incorporate analysis of the discursive frameworks that Latinos use to *talk* about their racial experiences as an important predictor of racial identification. Focusing on the understudied link between racial ideology and contemporary racial labeling among Mexican Americans, this book contributes both theoretically and empirically to our understanding of how Latinos navigate racial identification.

In the wake of the recent census demographics, there has been an upsurge of headlines across the country focusing on how an increasing presence of Latinos will shape the "new" face of America. However, while Mexican Americans and other Latinos are frequently cast in both the media and some scholarly publications as a new and emerging group in the United States, this portrayal elides a lengthy history of colonization and racialization experienced by Mexican Americans in this country (Gómez 2007; Murguía 1975). Understanding the contemporary racial position of Mexican Americans requires an examination of their complex racial history and the ways in which this history has contributed to the development of divergent and contradictory frameworks for articulating racial identities both in and outside the bounds of whiteness (Gómez 2007).

Mexican Americans: A Dual History of Racialization and Courting Whiteness

Are Mexican Americans a racial group? Sociologists commonly define race as a social construction of a group based on perceived biological difference, and ethnicity as a set of cultural attributes shared by a group with a common ancestry (Omi and Winant 1994; Cornell and Hartmann 1997). Cornell and Hartmann further argue that while these concepts share certain characteristics, race often operates as an assigned category that is both externally imposed and less flexible than ethnicity. They note (1997: 27), "Race has been first and foremost a way of describing 'others,' of making it clear that 'they' are not 'us'."

Historically in the United States, groups have been assigned racial identities in relation to whiteness. That is, racial identities have served the purpose of delineating who is white and therefore who reaps the benefits of citizenship, electoral participation, and access to educational and employment opportunities (Takaki 1993; Haney-Lopez 1996; Menchaca 2001). However, while racial assignment by others plays a crucial role in the development of racial identities, groups also assert racial identities that may or may not correspond to how others view and categorize them. Cornell and Hartmann (1997: 80) write:

> The world around us may "tell" us we are racially distinct, or our experiences at the hands of circumstances may "tell" us we constitute a group, but our identity is also the product of the claims we make. These claims may build on the messages we receive from the world around us or may depart from them, rejecting them, adding to them, or refining them.

Thus, identity construction involves a dynamic process whereby persons both receive messages about race from others and also actively interpret these experiences and create their own claims regarding their identity. How a group comes to make identity claims, and how successful they are in having those claims accepted by others, depends largely on structural and political circumstances, including especially the degree to which the group has been racialized (Cornell and Hartmann 1997).

For Mexican Americans, the roots of racialization in the United States can be traced to the Treaty of Guadalupe Hidalgo in 1848, when the current U.S. Southwest was acquired from Mexico. The United States promised citizenship to those Mexicans living in the colonized lands at a time when citizenship and legal rights were still contingent upon whiteness. Thus, through the treaty, Mexican Americans were afforded the legal rights of whites. However, as Laura Gómez (2007: 4) notes, "The central paradox was the *legal* construction of Mexicans as racially 'white' alongside the *social* construction of Mexicans as non-white and as racially inferior." Mexican Americans, who were often of racially mixed ancestry (European, Indigenous, and African), found themselves in an ambiguous category between the white and black races. Neil Foley (1997: 5) describes the historical situation of Mexican Americans in Texas:

> As a racially mixed group, Mexicans, like Indians and Asians, lived in a black-and-white nation that regarded them neither as black nor as white. Although small numbers of Mexican Americans—usually light-skinned, middle-class Mexican Americans—claimed to be white, the overwhelming majority of Texas whites regarded Mexicans as a "mongrelized" race of Indian, African, and Spanish ancestry. In Texas, unlike other parts of the South, whiteness meant not only not black but also not Mexican.

The identification of Mexican-ancestry persons as nonwhite served to keep Mexican Americans segregated and relegated to lower-wage employment, poor housing, and inferior resources. Throughout the Southwest, this segregation also meant the exclusion of Mexican Americans from many restaurants, movie theaters, and public pools, and the creation of separate "Mexican" schools (Montejano 1987; Almaguer 1994; Foley 1997; Menchaca 2001; Gómez 2007).

Mexican Americans fought this discrimination on multiple fronts. Initiating legal challenges, they demanded the rights of full citizenship and an end to segregation. One of the central tactics employed in these cases was the argument that Mexican Americans are racially white, a cultural or ethnic group that should not be viewed as a separate race. In some instances, they were able to persuade the courts with their claims that Mexicans were white or at least should be treated as if they were white, based on the Treaty of Guadalupe Hidalgo (Foley 1998). While Mexican Americans were certainly not the only group to use this strategy of combating racial discrimination with claims of whiteness, a combination of the legal loophole created by the Treaty of Guadalupe Hidalgo and the ability of Mexican Americans to evoke Spanish or other European ancestry made them more successful at these attempts than other racialized groups (Haney-Lopez 1996; Foley 1998). However, having been defined as white in some court cases did not equal being accepted as white by the general public, and in some ways this legal whiteness made it more difficult to combat racial discrimination. It is tricky to claim racial discrimination, for example, in a case where a Mexican is convicted by an all-white jury, if Mexicans are themselves legally white (Gross 2003; Sheridan 2003).

One organization known for utilizing this strategy of claiming whiteness to fight discrimination is the League of United Latin American Citizens (LULAC) that formed in Corpus Christi, Texas, in 1929. At the time, the largely middle-class, U.S.-born Mexican American members of this group often distanced themselves from both African Americans and Mexican immigrants in their efforts to mark themselves as white.[11] Not wanting to be racialized by the government, LULAC fought successfully to remove the racial category "Mexican" from the census, where it appeared for the first and only time in 1930 (Foley 1998).

Simultaneously, other efforts by Mexican American activists and organizations asserted a nonwhite identity, promoted Mexican Americans as a "race," and emphasized the population's indigenous roots. While this rhetoric was used in specific organizing efforts long before the 1960s and 1970s, it was during this time that embracing a "brown" or "mestizo/a" identity became the signature of many civil rights organizations. Groups such as the United Farmworkers of America and La Raza Unida political party formed, encouraging Mexican Americans to embrace their cultural heritage, working-class status, and racial identities in the struggle for social equality (J. García 1996; Marquez 2003). Thus, the history of Mexican Americans involves political mobilization against discrimination, utilizing divergent strategies of either claiming whiteness or asserting racialized identities (Marquez 2003).

Gómez (2007) questions whether the current identification with whiteness among Mexican Americans on the census might be similarly "defensive" in nature, reflecting a desire to resist racialization. However, no contemporary studies have examined the reasons Mexican Americans identify as "white" on these surveys, and in the absence of research on the topic, the dominant explanatory narrative remains that whiteness indicates assimilation and integration. *Mexican Americans and the Question of*

Race challenges this interpretation, demonstrating the ways in which the strategic use of whiteness in Mexican American communities converges with contemporary color-blind discourse to produce racial ideologies that evade asserting racial difference.

Survey Says: Latinos and the Census

As social scientists, we often rely on survey research, including the U.S. Census, to provide information about the racial demographics of the nation. These data assist us in gauging racial disparities and assessing the progress made toward ameliorating these differences. But while the census is currently used as a tool for assessing needs, allocating resources, and ensuring representation, the history of the federal measurement of race is far from benign. Indeed, the census does not merely reflect societal race relations but is inextricably linked with the construction of racial identities for various political ends. Identities based on African blood quantum (octoroon, quadroon, and mulatto) and "free or slave" categories for blacks reinforced racial identities based on biology and slave status (Anderson 1988; Lee 1993; Nobles 2000). The creation of categories for "Chinese," "Japanese," and "Mexican" were in part the result of increasing xenophobia and a desire to restrict immigration (Anderson 1988). In this way, formal racial and ethnic identities are created and reinforced in dialogue with the political context and power relations of a given time. Because political climates change, and minority groups actively create and resist labels, these identities are mutable, constructed and reconstructed for particular political ends (Padilla 1984; Espiritu 1992; Nagel 1994).

For over a century, the U.S. Census has grappled with appropriate strategies for enumerating the Latino population. Questions regarding foreign birth or foreign parentage were introduced in 1850, followed by a question concerning foreign-language usage that was instituted in 1890 (Chapa 2000). A "Mexican" racial group was added in the 1930 Census. However, as mentioned above, it was soon abolished due to vigorous opposition from LULAC, as well as protest from the Mexican government (Foley 1998). In 1950, a question regarding Spanish surname was added to the census for households in the Southwest. And in 1970, a Hispanic-origin question, separate from the race question, was introduced on the census "long form," an extended questionnaire distributed to select households. Since 1980, this question concerning "Hispanic/

Latino" origin has been listed on all census questionnaires,[12] and Latino responses to a separate race question largely reflect a split between those who identify as racially "white" and those who write in a response under the "other race" option (Rodríguez 1992, 2000; Tafoya 2004; Ennis et al. 2011).[13]

Latino racial responses on the census have been interpreted a number of different ways. Some scholars have read them as a reflection of phenotype, assuming that light-skinned Latinos may identify as "white," while dark-skinned Latinos label as "other race" or as "black" (Denton and Massey 1989). Others have argued that the history of racial mixing in Latin America, preferences for identification with national origin, or both lead Latinos to opt out of U.S. racial categories, marking "other race" (Tienda and Mitchell 2006). As previously noted, many others have suggested differences in racial self-identification may be indicative of levels of assimilation or inclusion in U.S. society (Yancey 2003; Tafoya 2004).

Analysis of national-level census data from both 1990 (Rodríguez 2000) and 2000 (Tafoya 2004) have found differences between Latinos who label as "white" and those who label as "other race" in terms of age, education, income, nativity, and language use. "White" Latinos are older, have higher socioeconomic status, and are more likely to be born in the United States and speak English (Rodríguez 2000; Tafoya 2004). However, Clara Rodríguez (2000) emphasizes that even among college graduates, those with higher incomes, and those born in the United States, a substantial number of Latinos still identify as "other race." Interviewing Latinos on the east coast, Rodríguez further explored the meaning of Latino racial "otherness" on the census (Rodríguez 2000). Her interviews with a mostly Dominican, Puerto Rican, and Ecuadorian sample reveal an understanding of race as a "cultural, social, and/or political concept" that differs from the largely biological mainstream U.S. conception of race, in which skin color is the primary determinant (Rodríguez 1992, 2000). Rodríguez suggests that this difference in the way in which Latinos see race leads many to mark "other race" and indicate Latino/Hispanic or their specific national origin on the census. The racial identities of her respondents did not always match their skin color but rather reflected this cultural identification and/or how they felt they were classified in the United States (Rodríguez 2000).

Roth (2010) reported similar results in her study of Dominican and Puerto Rican immigrants in New York, finding that these migrants' racial identities on the census did not match their phenotype or experiences with discrimination. Rather, her respondents struggled with competing definitions of race both from their home countries and the United States, often identifying in ways that conflicted with how they were seen and treated by others. Overall, both of these east coast-based qualitative explorations highlight that formal racial identification may have less to do with physical features and more with differing definitions of race. Both Rodríguez and Roth caution scholars not to interpret Latino racial responses as a direct reflection of skin color (Rodríguez 2000; Roth 2010).

However, other research utilizing national surveys that employ a racial question similar to the census has found that Latinos with lighter skin are more likely to label as "white" (Golash-Boza and Darity 2008; Frank et al. 2010). Golash-Boza and Darity (2008) further argue that skin color and experiences with differential treatment inform the process of racial labeling for Latinos. In their study, those with darker skin and those who reported experiences with discrimination were more likely to label as "black" or "Latino/Hispanic." Moreover, relying on these surveys, Golash-Boza (2006) reports that Latinos who are darker skinned and those who report discrimination are also less likely to identify as "American."

There are a few explanations for these conflicting findings. First, research suggests a great deal of regional variation in factors influencing racial labeling. Texas, for example, has the largest percentage of Mexican Americans who identify as racially "white" on the census (two-thirds, compared with roughly half at the national level).[14] In my research using 2000 census data, I found that whereas a national analysis of census data for Mexican Americans showed higher income to be associated with self-labeling as "white," Texas Mexican Americans in the lowest income groups were most likely to do so (Dowling 2004). Moreover, while Spanish language use has been linked to identification as racially "other" (Tafoya 2004), Texas Mexican Americans who spoke Spanish at home were about as likely to label as "white" as those who did not, at 63 and 65% respectively (Dowling 2004).[15]

Telles and Ortiz (2008) find further evidence of the importance of context. Using a racial question similar to the census, they report that Mexican Americans in San Antonio are over five times more likely to identify as white than their counterparts in Los Angeles. In fact, it is not skin color or experiences with discrimination but residence in Texas that is the only significant predictor of labeling as "white" in the study.[16] Their findings also show that the influence of skin color itself in the process of socioeconomic assimilation is also highly context specific. While previous research utilizing national-level data has shown skin color to be correlated with income and educational differences among Mexican Americans (Telles and Murguía 1990; Murguía and Telles 1996), Telles and Ortiz (2008) do not find this to be the case. They argue that other cues such as surname and neighborhood of residence may be enough to signify racial group membership in areas like San Antonio and Los Angeles that have such large Mexican populations, making skin color less predictive of socioeconomic outcomes.

A second factor that may account for the differences in findings regarding the relationship between skin color, experiences with discrimination, and formal racial labeling is the context of the question itself. Identifying one's race on a census form that is mandated by the U.S. government may be perceived very differently by respondents than answering any other survey: the question becomes about how they would like the government to see them rather than which label they personally prefer. Recall, for example, that Eddie Martinez felt obligated to answer "white" based on a legal definition of Mexican Americans as racially white. If he were asked for his preferred racial label during any other survey, he might have responded quite differently.

Also related to methodology, differences in how respondents define and report discrimination in surveys may further explain these divergent findings. For example, I find that Mexican Americans in Texas who strongly wish for others to view them as "Americans" identify as racially "white" and downplay their experiences with discrimination using color-blind discursive strategies. Individuals who detailed extreme episodes of racial prejudice earlier in the interview would later tell me that "No," they had not experienced discrimination. Hence, an important question emerges: Do Latinos who experience less discrimination identify more as "American" (Golash-Boza 2006), or do those who assert their "American" identities minimize their experiences with racism in line with their desire to project this American and/or "white" identity? It is likely that both statements hold true for individuals dependent upon a number of factors. To date, however, there has been very little research that explores exactly how Latinos define and talk about their experiences with discrimination and how this may impact racial labeling.

Research has examined multiple contextual variables as they relate to racial "otherness," but few studies incorporate any discussion of Latino whiteness (O'Brien 2008).[17] Moreover, scholarship in this area has focused primarily on Caribbean and South American Latinos on the east coast (Rodríguez 2000; Roth 2010). Mexican Americans constitute nearly two-thirds of Latinos in the United States, and both the racial discourse in Mexico and Mexican Americans' history of racial classification in the United States differ substantially from that of Caribbeans and South Americans. Thus, *Mexican Americans and the Question of Race* helps to fill a significant void in research on Latino racial labeling both by exploring the meanings of whiteness and racial "otherness" among Mexican Americans and Mexican immigrants from multiple communities and by linking their racial responses to the strategies or frameworks they use to talk about their racial experiences.

Research Design

This book draws on in-depth interviews with eighty-six Mexican-origin respondents from three very different locations in Texas: the Dallas/Fort Worth Metroplex (DFW), Del Rio, and Mission/McAllen. Examining racial labeling practices in three communities further illuminates how multiple contextual factors, including local histories, racial demographics, and geographies, contribute to the formation of racial identities. For example, while there are many places where Mexican Americans are racially profiled as "foreign," the U.S.–Mexico border is a site where the boundaries between "Americans" and "Mexicans" are policed in very concrete and systematic ways (Goldsmith et al. 2009). This seems to contribute to a heightened need to assert "American" identity. In the context of Del Rio and Mission/McAllen, both on the U.S.–Mexico border, citizenship becomes key in how Mexican Americans situate themselves on the racial ideology continuum, as "white/American" in opposition to "other/foreign."

Mapping Latino racial identification on the census by county, I find over 80% of Latinos in most Texas border counties identify as racially "white," a finding that no other study has documented. Figure 1.1 uses county-level data for Texas from the most recent 2010 Census. The darker areas are places where a higher proportion of the Latino population identified as "other" race, and lighter areas are locations where more Latinos selected "white." According to the census, the specific percentages of Latinos identifying as "white" in each of my three research sites are 54% (DFW), 84% (Del Rio), and 88% (Mission/McAllen). My results clearly show a pattern whereby Latinos along the U.S.–Mexico border are more likely to identify as white than in other parts of the state. This map reveals

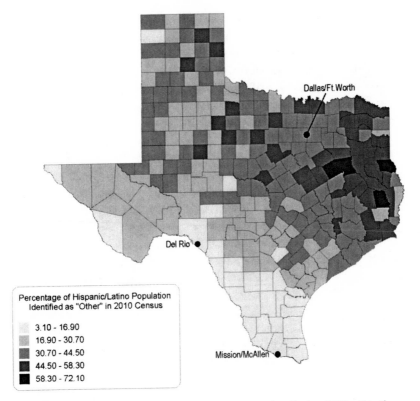

Figure 1.1. Percentage of Hispanic/Latino population identified as "Other" in the 2010 Census.

how even state-level analysis can obscure important variations, further highlighting the need for analysis of multiple locations.

I chose these three sites as they allow the examination of racial identification within very different local contexts. While all three areas have long-standing and overwhelmingly Mexican-origin Latino communities,[18] they vary in population size, racial composition, specific community histories, and geographic proximity to the Mexican border. The DFW Metroplex is a large, racially diverse urban area in North Texas with a current population of over 4 million, including a sizeable number of Latinos (34%), non-Hispanic whites (Anglos) (42%), African Americans (19%), and a smaller percentage of Asians (5%). DFW includes a range of small cities and subdivisions that span from Fort Worth to Dallas, including neighborhoods that are predominately white, black, Mexican origin, and Asian, as well as many racially mixed areas. The substantial proportion of African Americans in particular informs how Mexican-origin DFW residents define their racial identities, as they must negotiate their racial position relative to this highly racialized group. DFW is a crucial research site not only because of this racial diversity but also because it contains one of the largest Mexican American populations in the country. Indeed, nearly one out of every five persons of Mexican ancestry in the state of Texas lives in the Dallas-Fort Worth area.[19]

The drive from DFW to my second field site, the South Texas towns of Mission and McAllen, requires approximately nine hours and spans more than 530 miles. The cities of Mission and McAllen are located just across the border from Reynosa, Mexico, in the lower Rio Grande Valley of South Texas. The valley is a four-county, largely Mexican-origin area along the southern tip of Texas. Both cities are located in Hidalgo County, which is composed primarily of Latinos (90%), with a smaller percentage of non-Hispanic whites (9%), and very minimal African American presence (.4%).[20] Hidalgo County is also one of the largest home bases for Mexican migrant workers. Racial and ethnic distinctions in these border towns are primarily focused on the differentiation between Mexican immigrants, more established Mexican American families, and Anglos (Richardson 1999). Such close proximity to the border emphasizes the distinction between "American" and "Mexican" identities for residents in these communities.

Del Rio is also located on the Texas-Mexico border, but it is over 320 miles northwest and approximately a six-hour drive from the Mission/McAllen area. Del Rio is about 180 miles directly west of San Antonio and just across from Ciudad Acuña, Mexico. The total population is 33,867 persons, of whom 80% are Latino, and 18% are non-Hispanic white. Like most border towns in South Texas, the area is overwhelmingly Mexican origin and Anglo. However, Del Rio has a military base that draws in other populations, including African Americans and Asians. While the percentages of these groups are still quite small, 1% and .4% respectively, the town is more diverse than most along the South Texas border.[21] The presence of a small, but notable, African American community, as well as the town's location on the Mexican border, makes Del Rio a particularly interesting place to examine the contours of Mexican American and Mexican immigrant racial identification. Additionally, as mentioned earlier in the chapter, Del Rio is a historically important place in discussions of Mexican American racial identity, as the location of the first-ever school desegregation case involving Mexican Americans.

Study Participants

From 2002 to 2007 I interviewed 26 people from Mission/McAllen, 30 from Del Rio, and 30 from the Dallas/Fort Worth area.[22] The interviews were conducted in English or Spanish, whichever language was most comfortable for the respondent. Most used predominantly English with some Spanish words or phrases; fifteen of the interviews were conducted completely in Spanish.[23] The interviews were recorded for transcription, and pseudonyms were given to ensure anonymity. My respondents were gathered from several sources: community organizations and events, churches, and local gathering places. I also asked respondents for referrals. Thus, it is a "snowball" sample that includes both those who participate in community and public events and those who do not.

The study includes 42 men and 44 women, ranging in age from 18 to 81 and reflecting a diversity of educational and occupational characteristics. Some work in lower-level employment sectors, including construction, food service, housekeeping, manufacturing, and utility repair, while others are in sales, secretarial jobs, and managerial positions. Still others work as police officers, teachers, nurses, and business owners. I interviewed both immigrants and native-born Mexican Americans, including persons from a range of generational backgrounds. Overall, about one-quarter of respondents are immigrants, just over 40% are second generation, and one-third are third generation or beyond.

Aware that the background of the interviewer may influence responses, I identified myself before each interview as of Mexican ancestry, born and raised in Texas. I wanted to mark myself as an insider, a member of the community, but did not want to influence their responses by using a label such as "Mexican American" or "Chicana." Respondents were shown 2000 Census forms (which included racial options identical to those of the most recent 2010 Census). They were directed to questions for Hispanic origin and race and asked what they would answer and why. I asked not only for their own response but also how they would answer for other family members in the household. I further inquired about the labels they prefer to use in their day-to-day lives, what they would normally use to identify themselves, and whether this corresponded with their census form choice. I also asked about any associations they had with a variety of terms used to describe persons of Mexican ancestry (Mexican, Mexicano, Mexican American, Chicano, Hispanic, Latino, Tejano) and in what context, if any, they would use these labels.

The interviews averaged from 1 to 1.5 hours and included basic questions of demographics and family/personal migration history, as well as open-ended questions about family/social networks, Spanish-language use, political involvement, positive and negative associations with one's heritage, and relationships with other racial groups. I took notes on physical appearance, including skin color, and the presence of other cues such as accents. I also asked detailed questions about how they were perceived and categorized by others, what their experiences and strategies were for dealing with discrimination, and what costs and benefits they associated with their Mexican ancestry. For a more detailed discussion of the methodology and a table summarizing the demographics of the respondents, see the Appendix.

Outline of the Book

In Chapter Two, I introduce my theoretical framework, the racial ideology continuum. The continuum ranges from "color-blind" discursive frameworks in which respondents minimize race, to strong anti-racist ideologies, with multiple nuanced positions between these poles. In the chapter, I focus on those persons on the "color-blind" side of the continuum. These Mexican Americans identify as "white" on the census and distance themselves from African Americans and immigrants in their desire to project an American identity. "White" Mexican Americans often detail painful stories of racial discrimination and at the same time minimize these experiences. I argue that while utilizing similar narratives, these respondents espouse a color-blind ideology that is fundamentally different from that of European Americans. While the latter group uses this ideology to justify their racial privilege and higher social position, most Mexican Americans in the study use it as a defensive strategy to cope with discrimination.

Chapter Three focuses on Mexican Americans who fall on the other side of the continuum, identifying as "other race." As discussed earlier, Clara Rodríguez argues that many Latinos see race as a "cultural, social and/or political concept" that differs from the more biological definition of race in mainstream U.S. culture. "Other race" Mexican Americans in the study did make cultural assertions of race, but they often expressed a racial self-understanding based more on differential treatment. Rather than aligning themselves with whiteness, they asserted pride in their cultural heritage, which often served as a "counter-frame," or a way of resisting the dominant "white racial frame" (Feagin 2010). Moreover, "other race" Mexican Americans were more likely to align themselves with immigrants and situate themselves alongside African Americans. Finally, whereas the overwhelming majority of "white" respondents did not label in a way that corresponded to how others saw them, nor how they asserted themselves in daily life, most "other race" respondents wrote in a label that did reflect these realities. These findings reveal the key importance of external classification and the persistence of discrimination in shaping Mexican American racial identity.

Chapter Four focuses on Mexican immigrants' racial identification. The national discourse of race in Mexico relies on an understanding of Mexicans as a mestizo people composed of a mixture of Spanish and Indian ancestry (Doremus 2001; Sue 2013). Immigrants in the study typically identified their race as "Mexicano/a" first and foremost. However, some adopted "Hispanic," a category they understood to be assigned to them in United States. A few Mexican immigrants also relied on their prior social standing in Mexico in their decisions to identify racially as "white" or "other race." Finally, some immigrants who spent more time in this country relied on U.S. racial constructs, positioning themselves relative to African Americans and/or drawing on experiences with racial classification in the United States.

Chapter Five explores the contextual ways in which both Mexican Americans and Mexican immigrants identify themselves in daily interactions. I asked respondents how they identify most frequently, and then asked about various labels (Mexican, Mexicano/a, Mexican American, Hispanic, etc.), what were their associations with these labels, and if they would use them in any or every context. Overall, most U.S.-born interviewees identify primarily with the terms "Hispanic" and "Mexican American," while immigrants typically prefer "Mexicano/a," and sometimes adopt "Hispanic." However, these labels shift, dependent upon to whom they are speaking and in what language. Racial ideology further influences this process of identity assertions, as it informs with whom respondents wish to align themselves. My findings highlight both the contextual nature of racial and ethnic labeling and reveal the ways in which the "panethnic" terms "Hispanic" and "Latino" vary in their meanings regionally and even based on nativity within the same national-origin group.

I conclude in Chapter Six by expanding on the implications of this research for understanding Latino racial and ethnic identities. I emphasize the central role of racial discrimination in contributing not only to identification with racial "otherness" but also to how and why people assert white identities. My findings demonstrate the ways in which the local history of a strategic use of whiteness in Mexican American communities converges with contemporary discourses of color-blind racial ideology to minimize the importance of racial discrimination. I argue that while the color-blind discursive frameworks used by my Mexican American respondents are fundamentally different from those of European Americans, the effect of these strategies can be similarly detrimental in undermining efforts to organize against racial injustice.

"I'm white 'cause I'm an American, right?": The Meanings of Whiteness for Mexican Americans

Miguel Gonzalez, introduced in the first chapter, marked "white" for his race on the census, explaining, "'cause I'm an American, right?" This link between whiteness and American identity is a powerful one for my respondents, and understanding the complex connection between their claims to whiteness and the racial ideology they espouse requires a deeper examination. Classic sociological theories based on European migration conceived of assimilation into the dominant Anglo culture in stages, with the eventual endpoint being fixed, acculturated, white American identities (Park 1950; Gordon 1964). The emergence of whiteness as a social identity category in the United States, however, is as much a story of the creation and maintenance of racial ideology as it is one of cultural and structural assimilation. Various European immigrant groups came to be accepted as racially white by deliberately adopting a rhetoric of white supremacy that involved the degradation of blackness (Roediger 1991; Ignatiev 1995; Hale 1998; Feagin 2010). As Toni Morrison (1993: 57) notes, "In race talk the move into mainstream America always means buying into the notion of American blacks as the real aliens. Whatever the ethnicity or nationality of the immigrant, his nemesis is understood to be African American."

Joe Feagin (2010) argues that racism against African Americans and other racialized minorities remains deeply embedded in our national psyche as a fundamental component of what it means to be white in America. While Jim Crow–style segregation is no longer practiced, its legacy lives on in how we perceive and define race and inequality. Feagin provides a detailed examination of the emergence of what he terms the "white racial frame," a racial ideology that encompasses racialized stereotypes, narratives, images, emotions, and discriminatory practices that continue to shape American culture. Components of this framework include belief in the inherent superiority of whites, the devaluation of African Americans and other racialized minorities, and the minimization of both past and contemporary racial discrimination. According to Feagin, adherence to the white racial frame may involve explicit espousal of white supremacy but can also operate through an equally problematic "color-blind" ideology. This ideology discounts racism by emphasizing a deliberate nonrecognition of race (Frankenberg 1993; Gallagher 2003; Bonilla-Silva 2010; Feagin 2010). However, white Americans' denial of race masks underlying racist beliefs that continue to underpin and promote discrimination.

Eduardo Bonilla-Silva (2001, 2010) has conducted extensive research on the discursive functions of color-blind racial ideology and outlines four primary frames. The first ideological frame, abstract liberalism, uses the rhetoric of equal opportunity and meritocracy to explain inequality. According to this logic, whites are found in positions of higher social standing and success due to their stronger work ethic and better values. Affirmative action, therefore, is considered unfair preferential treatment and anti-egalitarian. The second frame of color-blind ideology, naturalization, claims that racial separation is a natural outcome because groups simply gravitate toward their own race. Thus, the practice of racial segregation is "just the way it is," inevitable. This discursive strategy frequently argues that racial minorities separate themselves, thus contributing to and enforcing segregation, and ignores the historical and structural factors that create and perpetuate discrimination. The third frame, cultural racism, uses "cultural" explanations for racial inequality such as, "Mexican Americans do not value education." The emphasis on culture in lieu of race allows speakers to claim they are not making racist statements but only observations of cultural difference. Finally, the fourth frame that Bonilla-Silva describes is the minimization of racism. Whites often describe racism as in the past, no longer a central factor affecting life chances, and they say that people of color should move on. According to this view, people who talk about race are the only ones being racially divisive (Bonilla-Silva 2010).

Color-blind racism has been studied primarily among white Americans, but it has also been found in the narratives of people of color, as they too are socialized within the white racial frame (Bonilla-Silva 2010; Feagin 2010). For example, Bonilla-Silva (2010) found some use of color-blind ideology among African Americans, although their use of such ideological frames was far less common compared with whites in the study. Few studies, however, have explored the use of color-blind ideology in Latino populations, and those that do focus primarily on the middle class. Feagin and Cobas (2008) found that many of their middle-class Latino respondents espoused elements of the white racial frame, discounting the significance of race when presented with vignettes about problematic interracial encounters. Similarly, in her study of racial identities among middle-class Asian Americans and Latinos, Eileen O'Brien's (2008) respondents also minimized their experiences with discrimination, having learned that talking about racism and racial barriers counters the dominant culture's emphasis on meritocracy. She argues that because Asian Americans and Latinos continually face accusations of "foreignness," emphasizing racial discrimination in a society that insists on minimizing the significance of race is particularly risky for them, as it could lead to being cast as even more "un-American."[1]

In my study, I found that Mexican Americans of a variety of class backgrounds identified as racially "white" on the census, using color-blind racial ideology and assertions of whiteness in a similarly defensive fashion. Two central themes are present in these narratives. First, "white" Mexican Americans wish to be seen as simply American and have internalized an association between American identity and whiteness. Second, they believe that calling attention to racial differences and organizing based on race perpetuates racial division. For "white" Mexican Americans, part of vying for acceptance as American means adopting the rhetoric of whiteness, including the use of color-blind ideology. Yet not all respondents did so to the same degree.

The racial ideology continuum (see Figure 2.1) captures a range between color-blind or race-evasive ideology and anti-racist politics. All Mexican Americans in the study fit into one of six points on the continuum. However, as this is a continuum and not a set of discrete categories, there is some variability among respondents within each location. Moreover, racial ideology and identity can be fluid and changing throughout one's life. As respondents may have shifted their ideological stance over time, this location on the continuum represents their current ideological frame. I will discuss such shifts in ideology where applicable throughout the analysis. The three points at the "white" end of the continuum will be discussed in this chapter: Race is no barrier, Leaving racism in the past, and Race/racism is transient. The three points on the "other race" end of the continuum will be discussed in Chapter Three. As previously noted, Mexican immigrants are not included in this framework because the processes by which they articulate racial identities differ substantially from Mexican Americans, a topic to be discussed in detail in Chapter Four.

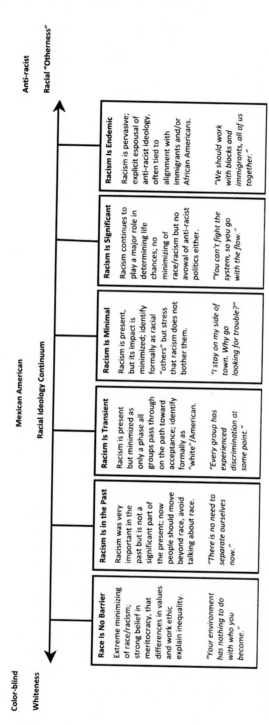

Figure 2.1. Racial ideology continuum.

Color-blind

Whiteness

Mexican American

Racial Ideology Continuum

Anti-racist

Racial "Otherness"

Race Is No Barrier

Extreme minimizing of race/racism; strong belief in meritocracy, that differences in values and work ethic explain inequality.

"Your environment has nothing to do with who you become."

Racism Is in the Past

Racism was very important in the past but is not a significant part of the present; now people should move beyond race, avoid talking about race.

"There is no need to separate ourselves now."

Racism Is Transient

Racism is present but minimized as only a phase all groups pass through on the path toward acceptance; identify formally as "white"/American.

"Every group has experienced discrimination at some point."

Racism Is Minimal

Racism is present, but its impact is minimized; identify formally as racial "others" but stress that racism does not bother them.

"I stay on my side of town. Why go looking for trouble?"

Racism Is Significant

Racism continues to play a major role in determining life chances; no minimizing of race/racism but no avowal of anti-racist politics either.

"You can't fight the system, so you go with the flow."

Racism Is Endemic

Racism is pervasive; explicit espousal of anti-racist ideology, often tied to alignment with immigrants and/or African Americans.

"We should work with blacks and immigrants, all of us together."

Of the twenty-eight Mexican Americans who identified as "white" on the census, six were in the most extreme "Race is no barrier" category. These respondents utilize multiple color-blind frames outlined by Eduardo Bonilla-Silva (2010), including especially a strong emphasis on abstract liberalism: they believe that individual efforts determine life chances. While they speak of discrimination, they rarely blame racism and instead highlight an individual ability to overcome. All six in this group were over forty years old and middle class. Their belief in meritocracy, while a defensive strategy to ward off racism, also served to justify their economic position. Ten respondents from a variety of economic backgrounds occupied the second category of "Leaving racism in the past." This group also uses multiple frames of color-blind ideology but not abstract liberalism. They understand racism to be an important factor determining past success, but they minimize its relevance today. These interviewees also believe that identification with racial labels and organizing based on race holds Mexican Americans back. One step further on the continuum, twelve "white" respondents were in the "Race/racism is transient" category. These individuals acknowledge the power of racism today, but they naturalize segregation and downplay their own encounters with discrimination. They often speak of race and/or racism as something transient, a phase that a group passes through on the way toward acceptance as American. Some even compare their experiences to those of European immigrants in our nation's history. However, these "white" Mexican Americans do not report less discrimination than "other" race respondents. They simply frame these racial encounters differently.

I will now turn to discussing each of these three points on the continuum in detail, focusing in-depth on individuals within each category. Examining a more detailed narrative of persons who exemplify each point on the continuum allows for incorporation of multiple contextual influences. Factors such as generation, location, class background, and experiences with racial classification radically shape both racial ideology and racial-label choice, and are a critical part of a nuanced examination.[2]

Race Is No Barrier: "Your Environment Has Nothing to Do With Who You Become"

Sixty-year-old Irene Hernandez greeted me warmly as I arrived at her office at a local business in Del Rio. She began our conversation by telling me a little about herself, including her many accomplishments. "I'm an achiever," she said. "Very soon in life I learned that I wanted to do something more than just live in the barrio. I wanted to do more than just be poor. I wanted to excel financially and academically as well, so I was always looking up." Irene was born and raised on the Mexican side of town in the barrio of San Felipe. Her parents had little formal education, and life growing up was marked by financial struggle. Yet, Irene credits her parents with instilling in her a desire to get a college education and succeed in an Anglo-dominated culture:

> My father stressed English. He would always say, "You are not going to compete with the Hispanic. You are not going to compete with the Spanish-speaking people. You are going to compete with the president of the United States. You are going to compete with the governor of the state of Texas, with the mayors, the attorneys, and the deans of colleges." We were five years old and my father said, "Irene, what are you going to do when you finish high school?" "Well . . ." [*Answering with a hesitant tone*] "No 'well!'" he would say to me, "Say after me, Irene: Daddy, I am going to college when I finish high school."

Neither of Irene's parents attended school past the fourth grade. Her parents were not immigrants to this country but fifth-generation Mexican Americans who were pushed out of the local schools due to economic hardship and discrimination. Irene explained how her father was not allowed to continue in school because his family could not afford the required clothing and fees. Such discriminatory policies were common throughout the Southwest at the time, existing alongside a system of segregation that placed Mexican Americans in separate schools (Montejano 1987). Since Mexican Americans were legally designated as white, segregation practices were allegedly based on linguistic and cultural deficiencies (Montejano 1987; Foley 2006). As a response to this segregation, many parents stressed using English as a strategy for upward mobility for their children. However, while Irene's parents emphasized English and academic achievement, they continued using Spanish at home and passed on a strong sense of cultural pride to their children.

Irene did complete her college degree and is now a successful businesswoman. But she did not sacrifice her heritage to get there. She speaks Spanish fluently, identifies strongly with her culture, and is an active member of the Mexican American community in Del Rio. Irene's husband is Mexican American as well, and the couple made sure to pass on cultural practices and the Spanish language to their children. Irene proudly marked "Mexican American" under the Hispanic-origin question on the census. However, when it came to identifying her race, Irene responded that while her culture is "Mexican," she is racially "white." She stated:

> Because as a race we are a white race. . . . Ignorance is the only thing that would cause anybody [who is Mexican American] to check anything else but white because that's what we are. We are not yellow; we are not black; we are not brown. There is no such thing as brown. All my children are fairer than you. . . . Are they brown? No, of course not. We've been here too long. We're just Americans. I mean I do not ever say that I'm Mexican. And the Mexicans hate us anyway.

Explaining her response, Irene says, "There is no such thing as a brown race." For her, white, black, and Asian ("yellow") are races, but "brown" is not. Irene was the only Mexican American in the study to discuss skin color in relation to checking "white" for her race, albeit that of her fair-skinned children rather than her own. Moreover, she insisted that while color differences among Mexican Americans can lead to tensions within the community, even the darkest Mexican American is still racially white. Furthermore, Irene continually linked whiteness to American citizenship and identity, saying she is "white" in part because, "We've been here too long. We're just Americans." Tensions with Mexican nationals ("The Mexicans hate us anyway . . .") further fuel her desire to identify as "white/American" in opposition to "other/foreign." For Irene, living in such close proximity to the Mexican border means daily interactions with Mexican immigrants who remind her that she is "American" and not "Mexican."

At first glance it might appear that Irene's story mirrors a traditional assimilation model, that over generations in the United States her family has "whitened" through attaining higher levels of education and increased class mobility, making her racial and ethnic background less salient. But further examination of Irene's experiences reveals far more complexity. Irene was very outspoken about growing up in a rigidly segregated community, describing the discrimination she faced as "severe." Even now, she says, people still assume she is less educated or intelligent because she is Mexican American. As a youth she wanted to fight this discrimination, and she started an organization to protest the exclusion of Mexican Americans from certain public recreational facilities in town. She relied on an argument that Mexican Americans are racially white, which was a common strategy of her generation (Marquez 2003). Her successful efforts further solidified her belief that arguing for civil rights for Mexican Americans on the basis of their whiteness is a strong strategy.

While Irene's identification with whiteness is rooted in her early experiences with protesting segregation, her comments also reflect multiple aspects of contemporary color-blind racial ideology. Irene credits her success to an ability to be "articulate," which she attributes to the values her parents taught her. She espouses abstract liberalism, including a meritocratic philosophy that individuals make their own fortune in the United States and that personal ambition and values are the most important factors in determining life chances. She asserted:

> Your environment has nothing in my opinion to do with what you become. I believe that [it's a result of] what your parents teach you inside those four walls. When you walk out of that door that's falling apart, but you look at it . . . Maybe it's an unrealistic way of thinking, but my daddy would always say, and my mom, "When you walk out of here, you are representing this entire family, and you are very intelligent; you are very beautiful." These are people that didn't even go to the fifth grade, and they were instilling self-esteem in us.

Irene also credits her success to her parents' emphasis on a strong work ethic, noting that they passed on positive values despite their own limited opportunities. In addition to abstract liberalism, Irene's statements also embody aspects of cultural racism in her emphasis on values as determining success and in her strict avoidance of racial terminology. Persons employing cultural racism avoid using the word "race," and instead use other words or expressions considered more palatable such as "culture" or in this case "environment."

Even when Irene describes the discrimination she and her family faced growing up as "severe," she never once attaches the terms "racism" or "racial discrimination" to those experiences. Moreover, while Irene was very active in fighting discrimination in her youth, and is currently involved in civic and other community groups, she would not join an organization based on her race or ethnicity. In our conversation, she explained:

> Irene: I don't believe in that. I just believe in rights, but I don't believe in organizing [based on that] . . . I don't belong to those things. I don't like that *la raza* garbage. To me it's just garbage. It's worked for the blacks but not for the Hispanic people.

JAD: Why not?

Irene: Because we are not bold like the negro, or the black. I don't know what you call them now. The Hispanics didn't have money. The blacks don't either, but they are very . . . [*she pauses, reflecting* . . .] The Hispanics have a lot more pride, I think.

Irene believes in "rights" but not in using a rhetoric of racial difference similar to African Americans to fight for those rights. Earlier in the interview, she commented extensively on her disdain for the word "Chicano," a term associated with civil rights organizing that employs a more race-based, nonassimilationist approach (Marquez 2003). Irene stated:

[When I hear Chicano,] I think of César Chávez. I think of low-class uneducated Mexican Americans. I think of rebellion. I think non-American, and the people that use . . . these words are ignorant. . . . Many of us in this area were so discriminated upon and hurt by the Anglo population. They hurt us why? Because they were ignorant, and they lacked the knowledge that their forefathers had come into Mexican land, dug holes, put the Mexican families, threw them in these pits and killed them. And that's how all these big ranches came about, by killing the owners. And the owners were humble peasants, Mexican peasants on *their* land because Tejas and Texas was *their* land. I say it not with vengeance, or with anger, but a sorrow that I will not live long enough to really talk about it. What is the truth about these lands . . . the Americans have been abusive to people from day one when they came from Europe. They were renegades. The Mexicans weren't renegades. This was their land. The Anglo population treated them like dirt. Chicano is an Anglo word as far as I am concerned. It's a slang word. I think we need to be proud to be Americans of Mexican descent and that our culture is a beautiful culture because American[s], the European, Anglo quote unquote have no culture. We do!

Irene's racial ideology is complex, and at times it seems contradictory. On the one hand, she is profoundly aware that Mexican Americans have a bitter history with discrimination. Yet, rather than linking this to systemic racism, she presents it as an issue of ignorance. Arguing that discrimination directed at Mexican Americans results from a "lack of knowledge" removes any structural dimension to the problem. This separation of racism from its structural complexity is another way that color-blind racial ideology operates: Racism is seen as the bigoted exception, a result of an individual choice to discriminate, and not a larger, pervasive societal problem (Gallagher 2003; Bonilla-Silva 2010).

Perhaps the most striking example of the color-blind logic in Irene's narrative is her belief that calling attention to race and racial differences is fundamentally "un-American." Irene has internalized an image that "American" means white and middle class, and she feels that drawing attention to working-class and immigrant populations within the Mexican American community weakens this image. One of the components of the naturalization frame of color-blind ideology is the argument that when racial minorities segregate themselves, they perpetuate racism (Bonilla-Silva 2010). Irene employs this framework in her staunch opposition to the use of a rhetoric of racial difference. Instead, she strongly advocates for a strategy of claiming whiteness and assimilating into American society through educational and class mobility. Notice, however, that she does not want Mexican Americans to lose their cultural heritage. Irene calls herself an "American of Mexican descent" or "Hispanic," terms that she feels emphasize her culture without differentiating her racially from the dominant white population.

The strategic element of Irene's approach is important. While she is adamant about self-labeling as "white" on the census, she could not think of a situation where she would ever identify herself as such in her daily life. Claiming whiteness is a tool for Irene, utilized primarily to assert a public racial identity with outsiders. Her race-evasive ideology is rooted in a history of courting whiteness but is also infused with a pervasive contemporary racial ideology that emphasizes the denial of race as the solution to racism.

Mari Bredahl, a teacher in her fifties living in the Dallas area, also uses a "Race is no barrier" color-blind rhetoric and assertions of whiteness. She and her parents, both Mexican Americans, were born in Texas. Her mother was the daughter of immigrants, while her father's family dates back at least three generations in Texas. Mari was also raised in an overwhelmingly Mexican and Spanish-speaking community, but unlike Irene's family, hers did not struggle financially. Her mother was a teacher, her father a businessman, and Mari expected to go to college. But, she was not at all prepared for the prejudice she would encounter once there. While aware of discrimination against Mexican Americans during her youth, she felt that growing up in a largely Mexican community had shielded her from this: "I knew it was out there, but in my neighborhood we just didn't feel it." However, the university she attended in central

Texas was overwhelmingly white, and Mari remembers vividly the overt bigotry she faced:

> Mari: And I saw discrimination there. I saw it on the signs. It said, "We refuse to serve Mexicans." I was horrified.
>
> JAD: Where were the signs?
>
> Mari: [They were] in the restaurants. I had never seen it before. I had never been discriminated against until then. And then, there was this incident. When I got to college, my roommate was a girl from [a] German background. . . . And when she saw me, that I was her roommate, she nearly died. I mean we didn't know each other. She just took one look at me and walked out of the room. And she went down and told the hall mother and had her room changed. . . . [Later] she ended up feeling so guilty and so bad. She told me, "I didn't want to share a room with a Mexican. I didn't know what you were going to be like." I mean it didn't bother me that much. I have a lot of self-confidence. Maybe for someone who did not have as much confidence it would bother them. . . . But [she] was a German and they are just racist.

Mari experienced a profound episode of racism when, on her first day at college, she was rejected by her roommate because of the color of her skin. It is an experience she remembers decades later. Yet Mari minimizes this incident, claiming that her self-confidence enabled her to overcome it. In addition to downplaying the impact of the event, in Mari's narrative, racism is discussed as a component of German culture, rather than a larger problem in U.S. society. Mari spoke of racism as an individual choice to discriminate, which, similarly to Irene, she attributes to ignorance. Again, this definition of racism further minimizes its structural power.

Mari checked "white" for her race on the census stating, "Because I'm Caucasian, and that includes all brown people." It became clear through further discussion that Mari is making a distinction between African Americans and all others. However, while Mari insists that she is racially white, she notes that she is not typically perceived as white by others, and further comments on how she has been classified formally as racially "other" in the past:

> Mari: I used to be an "other," way back early when we were young, we were "others." Now if you married like I did [her husband is Anglo] you weren't an "other" anymore. I was Ramirez, so that's a Mexican Ameri-

can. But when I walked down the aisle, I was no longer categorized by the government as Mexican American—I was no longer an "other." . . . Back thirty years ago, we were others. [The forms said,] "black," "white," or "other."

JAD: But you wouldn't put "other" now?

Mari: *No*, I've always thought that I was of the Caucasian race, of the white race. I never thought that I was not white.

JAD: But when you married, do you think it changed for you?

Mari: It changed for the government, the way they looked at me because my last name changed, not because I changed. I remained the same and I felt the same.

Mari clarified that she has always marked "white" on forms when given the option to self-identify. However, during her youth, school administrators and employers typically classified her as racially "other" on bureaucratic forms, due to skin color and surname. In fact, for many years the government used Spanish surnames as a measure of Hispanic identity in the Southwest (Chapa 2000). Therefore, Mari feels that after her last name changed, she became white in the eyes of the government. She admits, however, that she is unsure how she usually appears "on paper," with a common Spanish first name and a Swedish last name. But Mari is certain that others see her as Mexican American simply because of her skin color. She elaborated on her experiences:

As a teacher I always felt that I was scrutinized a lot closer than other teachers, and so I always had to dress better. I felt like I had to dress well so they wouldn't say, "Oh look, she's different." I felt that way. And just recently, about three or four years ago I felt like one of the parents did not like me because I was Mexican. . . . I felt like it was a discrimination thing. But I don't think that the school wanted to hear about it. And I felt very strongly that it was because I was Mexican and I don't deny it. And that is the thing—that I don't make it a quiet thing. My children [in class] know [that I am Mexican], and they know I speak Spanish. I speak Spanish to them sometimes.

Mari is very proud of her cultural background. In fact, she was vigilant about making sure that her son learned to appreciate his Mexican heritage and speak Spanish fluently. She brings this pride into the classroom, talking to her mostly Anglo students about Mexican culture, and even teaching them some Spanish words and phrases. She tells her students about the need to respect different "cultures," but she is very deliberate in instructing them that while cultural differences are important, race is irrelevant. "I teach them to be color-blind," she explained. When Mari's students take standardized tests, she goes over the instructions and emphasizes that the race question on the form is optional, saying, "Remember that race does not matter." "They can always tell at the office which tests come from my room," Mari said, "because all the race questions are left blank." Teaching her students not to identify racially is part of her strategy for combating discrimination. Again, this deliberate nonrecognition of race is a common trope of color-blind ideology (Gallagher 2003; Bonilla-Silva 2010).

Given that Mari advises her students to opt out of a racial identity, it may seem surprising that she herself answers the census race question. The distinction for Mari between formal identification and the ways in which she identifies in daily life is quite striking. She typically uses "Mexican American" or "Hispanic" to identify herself when speaking to others. Moreover, as her story above demonstrates, she does not keep her Mexican heritage "a quiet thing." Yet she was hesitant about checking "Mexican American" under the Hispanic-origin question on the census. She reluctantly said that she would "go ahead and put that if they really need to know," as long as she could still answer "white" for her race. Mari feels there is a stigma attached to checking "Hispanic" on forms. When asked if she would like to see a Hispanic option under the race question, she replied:

> No, because I think that you should be able to be taken for your own value—not just what your last name is. I mean it's nice that there is minority money and all this stuff, but I'm just saying that it does not matter as far as intelligence, if you are a good worker. We should all work for things.

Implicit in Mari's response is an understanding that labeling as racially Hispanic on a form means privileging race as a defining trait. Because Mexican Americans are stereotyped as less intelligent and industrious, Mari believes identifying as such could have implications for how she is seen by others. Marking "white" for her race on the census is a defense against these assumptions, a way to minimize attention to racial differences. This also illustrates a key aspect of color-blind ideology, where whiteness typically functions as the "unmarked" or "raceless" category. White European Americans often do not think of themselves as having a racial identity, identifying simply as "Americans." They then fault racial minorities for perpetuating racial divisions by taking on hyphenated American identities (e.g., "Why do they have to separate themselves? Why can't they just be Americans?") (Gallagher 2003). Mari internalizes this logic: for her, checking "white" is not constructing racial divisions but eliminating them. She espouses this raceless rhetoric, however, while simultaneously articulating a boundary between Mexican Americans and African Americans.

Similarly to Irene, Mari also employs the frame of abstract liberalism by stating that work ethic determines success. When Mari links identifying racially as Hispanic with affirmative action, saying that "minority money" is "nice" but that "we should all work for things," she is taking issue with the stigma she feels is attached to being labeled a racial minority. Also like Irene, Mari intensely dislikes the word "Chicano" and feels that it reinforces the notion that Mexican Americans are all laborers in the fields. Mari has struggled against this stereotype her whole life. As a Mexican American woman from a more middle-class upbringing, she has been told multiple times by Anglos (including her assigned college roommate) that, based on her appearance, they expected her to be someone quite different than who she is. This leads Mari to have conflicted feeling about affirmative action. When asked if she felt she ever benefited from her racial or ethnic background, she responded:

> No, I always missed all those things! [*Laughs.*] Well, I was on a scholarship, but it wasn't because I was Mexican American. No, I don't think so. Oh, you know, one of the schools did try to hire me because I was Mexican American and they needed some bilingual teachers, and I didn't choose them. *I* didn't choose *them*. They chose me because of that, but actually the person hiring me could not believe that I said, "No." He said, "We're talking about more money than you've ever seen." And that changed it for me. I would not work for them. How did he know how much money I had ever seen!

Mari is insulted that someone would assume that all persons of Mexican ancestry are working class. Like Irene, she argues that these stereotypes are based on ignorance but does not explicitly connect that ignorance to underlying structural racism. The story regarding her would-be college roommate was the only moment in the interview in which she ever used the word "racist." Irene and Mari acknowledge a great deal of discrimination in their lives, but they minimize these experiences by emphasizing that their self-confidence allows them to rise above such episodes. They both are very proud of their culture as Mexican Americans but reject a politics of racial difference in favor of deploying whiteness to counter discrimination.

Mexican Americans in this "Race is no barrier" position on the continuum are all currently middle class, but they do not believe they achieved whiteness through social mobility. Rather, they adamantly argued that all Mexican Americans (or, in Mari's opinion, "all brown people") are racially white, not just those who have achieved a higher social class standing as they have. They believe working-class and darker-skinned Mexican Americans are also white, and they expressed frustration about lower-class, less-educated Mexican Americans who continue to use a rhetoric of race.[3] They feel that these individuals should stop calling attention to their race (and lower-class status) and focus on upward mobility as the way to combat discrimination.

Like middle-class white European Americans, persons on this extreme end of the continuum use abstract liberalism and other frames of color-blind ideology to justify their higher social position. They credit their accomplishments to hard work and imply that others can get ahead in the same way. Yet, despite their achieved class status, they still face discrimination in their daily encounters. While they would like to be seen as white (or as "American"), others classify them as nonwhite and make assumptions about them based on stereotypes about Mexican Americans. Irene, for instance, said that people doubted that she could have a college degree and would ask, "Are you really from here?" Mari relayed similar experiences. Those in this position on the continuum spoke of wanting whites to recognize that they are "different" and not like stereotypical Mexican Americans because *they* value education, *they* work hard. These experiences with discrimination make their use of color-blind ideology fundamentally different from European Americans, as the emphasis on meritocracy is part of a defensive strategy they use because others have questioned their abilities and work ethic. Unlike white European Americans, they do not claim not to "see" race; they simply want others not to see them as racially different and inferior. Thus, the rhetoric of whiteness and color-blind racial ideology are tools they use as an attempt to evade racial discrimination.

All six who used this "Race is no barrier" framework are over forty years old, have lived through a history of rigid segregation in Texas, and have experienced overt forms of racism such as Mari's incident with her college roommate. In fact, nearly all Mexican Americans in this age group that I interviewed (both those who identified as "white" and those who selected "other race") described experiences with school and residential segregation, of being refused service at restaurants, or of not being allowed to use public recreational facilities. This history of Jim Crow–style segregation informs contemporary racial labeling for both older and younger Mexican Americans who hear these stories from parents and grandparents. The next point on the continuum, "Leaving racism in the past," further reveals how racism in the past shapes how Mexican Americans construct racial ideologies and identities today.

Leaving Racism in the Past: "There Is No Need to Separate Ourselves Now"

Miguel Gonzalez, mentioned in the introduction to this chapter, is a janitor in his midforties who grew up in an impoverished *colonia* on the outskirts of Mission. His mother was a Mexican immigrant, and his father was a Texas-born Mexican American. Miguel has many siblings, and his family worked picking crops in the fields throughout his youth. He managed to finish high school, but he admits having to work so hard made getting an education a challenge. As a migrant worker, he also faced a lot of discrimination growing up, including once being refused service at a restaurant. But he says, "Nowadays, it's very different. The government protects us." Miguel believes we should now "leave the past in the back, and leave the bad aside." He views discrimination as a significant part of his past but feels it is more important to focus on the good things in his life. He has a strong faith in God and believes he is called to forgive these incidents. "I always think positive," he said.

Miguel works long hours and spends his free time with his wife, who is also Mexican American, as well as visiting his parents and siblings who live nearby. When I asked if he or anyone in his family had ever been involved in any organizations or clubs in the community, he replied:

> We were lucky if we had food on our table. [*Laughs.*] No, we were just normal people, working and still [are]. . . . When César Chávez . . . he came here to the valley . . . back then we had *las huelgas* [the strikes], that's what we called them then. But it was like if you don't work you don't eat. [It was as] simple as that. We had to work. That was our life . . .

we had César Chávez and La Raza Unida and all that, but we didn't pay attention to that.

Miguel sees himself and his family as hard workers who feel that it is important to "go with the flow" and not make waves. "I work. Never say no to the boss and be happy. Live a simple life," he said. For Miguel, drawing attention to racial discrimination means creating problems that he deems too risky while living so close to poverty.

Miguel identifies strongly with his Mexican heritage. He speaks Spanish fluently, lives in a working-class, largely Mexican neighborhood, and has primarily Mexican American friends. However, while he marked "Mexican American" under the Hispanic-origin question on the census, he says he prefers to be considered simply "American." When Miguel selected "white" on the racial identification question, stating, "'Cause I'm an American, right?" the questioning tone of his response belied the reality that this is not how he is typically seen and classified by others. Miguel has a dark-brown complexion, and while walking the streets of his hometown, he is often mistaken for an immigrant. Like Irene who also lives in a border town, claiming whiteness on the census is a way to mark himself as "white/American" as opposed to "other/foreign." His identification with whiteness is also an extension of his philosophy of coping with discrimination by "going with the flow." In this case, that means publicly adopting the racial identity of the dominant majority.

Miguel's belief that the best solution to deal with racism is not to dwell on it, and his view that racism is primarily a problem of the past, both resonate with contemporary color-blind ideology (Bonilla-Silva 2010). But unlike the respondents in the more extreme "Race is no barrier" category, Miguel's racial ideology does not serve to justify higher social class standing, as he is not middle class. Moreover, he does not utilize abstract liberalism to explain inequality. While he does believe all people can get ahead if they "work hard," he does not argue that race has not been a hindrance for him and for others, only that we should "leave it in the past." Miguel's narrative highlights how the contemporary use of assertions of whiteness to combat discrimination is a strategy that varies in terms of its motivation and uses among Mexican Americans. It is not simply a middle-class phenomenon. Rather, economic vulnerability can also lead persons to publicly profess alliance to the racial majority. As a working-class Mexican American, Miguel feels he cannot afford to "rock the boat" by asserting racial difference.

Like Miguel, Del Rio resident Petra Mancini believes that Mexican

Americans should move beyond their racial past and embrace "American" identities. A retired secretary and grandmother in her seventies, Petra grew up in a largely Mexican neighborhood. Her father was a ranch hand whose family dates back many generations in South Texas, and her mother was a Mexican immigrant who took care of the children. Petra has a light-olive skin tone, which in a town like Del Rio is usually interpreted as indicating Mexican origin. However, through her marriage she acquired an Italian last name, and occasionally strangers will ask about her ancestry. Growing up, Petra went to segregated "Mexican" schools and never saw college as an option. While she spoke of segregation in her youth, later in the interview when I asked whether she had ever been discriminated against, she said, "No, I never have experienced it, but I know other people who have." Petra spoke of "discrimination" as racial slurs directed at individuals or other isolated incidents of bigotry occurring in the past. Like Miguel, she feels that it is time to move on. She checked the "Mexican/Mexican American" box under the Hispanic-origin question, because "my ancestry is Mexican," although like Miguel she prefers to call herself simply "American." Petra then marked "white" for her race, elaborating on her desire for persons to turn away from racial and ethnic labels in favor of adopting an American identity. She said:

> I dislike that term [Mexican American] because we are from here, so we are Americans. Why put yourself in a label? When you think about all the discrimination back many years ago, and then we joined the schools together. And now the people, the Mexican Americans and the African Americans, they try to separate themselves again. So to me that is just separating themselves. We are Americans.

Petra refers to the history of rigid segregation in Del Rio and the subsequent consolidation of the separate Anglo and Mexican school districts. She believes such discrimination is an important component of her community's history but not a contemporary issue. She argues that when people call attention to racial differences, they are bringing on problems for themselves. Petra calls these persons who organize under a politics of racial differences "troublemakers." Similarly to Mari and Irene from the previous section, Petra does not see marking "white" as constructing a racial barrier. For her, whiteness is synonymous with American identity; it is identifying as nonwhite that is separatist and racially divisive. Moreover, Petra minimizes racial discrimination, never actually using the word "racism" during the interview, and stating that she has never faced discrimination due to her ethnic or racial background. Again, this was in spite of her earlier discussion of pervasive segregation and attendance at separate "Mexican" schools in her youth. This minimization of discrimination resonates with Eileen O'Brien's (2008) work on middle-class Latinos and Asian Americans, but it also highlights how persons like Miguel and Petra, who are more economically vulnerable, may feel they have more to lose if the dominant majority sees them as "un-American."

The majority of those in this position on the continuum are older individuals who referred to the more extreme prejudice they faced growing up and explained how today is not as bad. They tend to see present racial incidents as isolated episodes of bigotry, remnants of history. However, some younger individuals also use this framework of "Leaving racism in the past."

Joe Salinas is a salesman in his thirties living in Fort Worth. Joe was raised in a lower middle–class neighborhood in South Fort Worth, with a mixture of whites and Mexican Americans. He is fourth-generation Mexican American, and his parents both worked low-wage jobs during his youth. Joe was the first in his family to attain a college degree. He has been working in sales at a local department store now for many years. His wife is a Mexican immigrant, and he says they have been helping each other improve their respective Spanish and English skills. Joe usually identifies as Mexican American or Hispanic in daily life, but he put "white" for his race, stating that he is "American" and not "Mexican." His brown skin color, however, makes it difficult to be seen by others as simply "American." At the store where Joe works, he says customers frequently direct racial slurs at him when angry about store policies. In most cases he does not believe they mistake him for an immigrant but rather have negative stereotypes of Mexican Americans in general. When I asked how he responds to these incidents, he replied, "I just tell them I'm sorry. . . . I don't have any anger, I just walk away. [It's] their ignorance." Joe says he shrugs off such episodes: "It's their problem, not mine." He further explained that he knows that his parents and grandparents faced far worse prejudice, and he feels what he experiences is only a shadow of what they encountered in their daily lives. Like Miguel and Petra, Joe believes it is time to move on and stop focusing on racial differences and that the best way to combat this discrimination is to not dwell on it.

Ruben Perez also feels we should leave racism in the past. Ruben is in his midtwenties and lives in Mission, where he was born and raised. His mother's family dates back many generations in South Texas, and his father was an immigrant from Central Mexico. When Ruben and I spoke, he was working part-time at a library in a neighboring town, having just returned to the Rio Grande Valley after completing his master's degree at Iowa State. Before his stint in the Midwest, Ruben had completed his degree at a local college and had never lived outside South Texas. Ruben said, "I think before when I was attending college here, I was always around Hispanics. . . . I would visit friends that were living in Austin, [but] I could never be comfortable talking to a white person. I always felt very insecure. I always felt like I couldn't talk to them." Ruben says going to Iowa for graduate school changed that, as it forced him to make friends with a variety of people, including many whites and Asians in his program. There, he said people were curious about his cultural background, and he learned to be comfortable around other racial groups. He feels strongly that one of the biggest mistakes Mexican Americans make is separating themselves from others. He spoke about how collections in some libraries in the area are divided by ethnicity and how he feels Mexican Americans need to stop doing this and stop separating themselves:

> It's something we need to blend—these collections together and—yeah, I guess just bring together different ethnicities. The way of thinking has to change. So in a way I feel as if by doing this, by attending to only a certain race and whatnot, we segregate ourselves. These are the people who started the nation [referring to famous white families, landowners in South Texas]. There are stories about how racist they were, but that is in the past. We've learned from that and we've moved on. But it's still a big part of history. And then, their families are still here. These are people who we need to bring [in], and we need to learn from, and vice versa. So, but yeah, I've seen it where it's just Hispanics. People come over here, more Hispanics and more Hispanics, people of Mexican descent—then, we just segregate ourselves. . . . Um, but I guess that's one thing that I learned living in Iowa. It goes back to the—you know, as a Hispanic, you almost, it becomes something more, you start to open yourself more, because you begin to know so many other people. . . . [I say,] "Oh yeah, I'm Hispanic"—that doesn't matter anymore. I find myself down here defending myself more as not being Mexican. [And I say,] "I'm not a Mexican, I'm a Hispanic." But when I was up there, it doesn't matter. I'm *somebody*, not just Hispanic.

In addition to stating very clearly that he thinks of racism as a part of the past and that Mexican Americans should stop separating themselves, Ruben also speaks of the freedom he felt in being seen as "something more" than Hispanic. Ruben contrasts this to his experiences in Texas, where he is frequently mistaken for an immigrant. Texas has immigration checkpoints located on routes leaving South Texas. When Ruben is traveling north to San Antonio or Austin, he is usually stopped and interrogated, his citizenship questioned. He says:

> I cannot survive the checkpoints. I'm always pulled over. . . . We go through checkpoints going to Austin, it never fails. . . . They'll ask, "American citizens?" And that—it's very embarrassing. One time, I was traveling with my in-laws, and I was in the front seat with my father-in-law, who was driving, and they—the lady walks up and she's like, "Carlos?" She knew him, she knew my father-in-law. . . . And she looks in the back, and she sees my mother-in-law, my wife, and her sister, and she looks at me, and I'm serious she goes, "Who are you?" And I was like, "Oh my name is Ruben." [She asked,] "American citizen?" And I was like, "yes." She goes, "Can I see your ID?" . . . They all knew [my in-laws]. I told them before I don't survive checkpoints. It's worse when going to Mexico. It *always* happens. And after the legal checkpoint we're laughing for a good a mile and a half because it doesn't fail. I mean, one day I'm gonna wear a poncho and a big Mexican hat and that's when I'm really gonna pass [*laughs*]. . . .
>
> JAD: How do you feel about that? Does it bother you?
>
> Ruben: Oh, well you know it's gotten to a point where . . . [*pauses*] it does. It all depends 'cause it's gotten to the point where at least they're not pulling me over *constantly*. But I don't know what it is. . . . I've started to search my whole—my facial structure. And I think it's my eyes. A lot of Mexican nationals have eyes like mine.

These incidents have led Ruben to study his face in the mirror for clues as to why immigration officers see him as "illegal." He has a brown complexion, but he has noticed others with his skin color do not always get the same treatment. Ruben says that they do not seem to believe him when he says he is a citizen. Even when he presents his identification, he has been searched multiple times. The irony, he says, is that many times it is Mexican Americans who work at these checkpoints, and so he is often being questioned by his own people. It has gotten so bad that Ruben actually feels anxious when he leaves the valley. "I start practicing saying, 'American citizen, American citizen.' . . . It's crazy because I am from here! I think at some point I guess it's discriminating." Ironically, right after this comment, I followed up by asking about Ruben's experiences with discrimination, and he said that he has never really experienced it—that no one has ever given him a "bad attitude." Thus, despite his poignant stories of racial profiling, he still minimizes racism in his life.

Ruben's narrative highlights very specifically how contemporary border policing has an impact on U.S.-born Mexican Americans and can further contribute to their identification as racially white to assert American identity. However, Ruben's decision to mark "white" for his race was also related to the legacy of courting whiteness among Mexican Americans. Ruben explained that years ago a teacher had instructed him that Hispanics were not a race and that they should always check "white" officially on forms. Since high school he has followed her advice, assuming it to be correct. Interestingly, during the interview Ruben said that while he did check "white" in 2000, he thinks he might change his answer next time because "white" does not really describe him.

In sum, the ten persons in the "Leaving racism in the past" position on the continuum expressed an overwhelming sentiment that racism was primarily a part of our history and that "there is no need to separate ourselves now." All but one (Ruben) said they preferred to have the Hispanic-origin question separate from the race question on the census, allowing them to identify as Hispanic without separating themselves racially from other "Americans." Ruben, however, says he would identify racially as Hispanic if it were an option and that in the future he may do so under "other race." Ruben's comments on this resonate with those in the next group, defined by the belief that race/racism is transient.

Race/Racism Is Transient: "Every Group Has Experienced Discrimination at Some Point"

I met Teresa Garcia at a town meeting in Del Rio where people gathered to discuss the struggle for better salaries and benefits at a local establishment whose employees were primarily Mexican immigrant workers. Teresa, one of the key members of a local activist organization, was the event's main organizer. A college graduate, wife, and mother in her early forties, Teresa is self-employed. She and her husband, who is also Mexican American, own a successful family business in town. But Teresa's experiences with economic hardship growing up have made her especially sensitive to the plight of low-wage workers. Both of her parents were migrant workers, and she grew up on the Mexican side of town in the barrio of San Felipe. Her father is a second-generation Mexican American, and her mother is an immigrant from Ciudad Acuña, Mexico.

Teresa marked "white" for her race on the census because "I don't see Hispanic or Mexican American, so white is what I would have to put." Teresa has a dark-brown complexion and speaks both Spanish and English fluently. She identifies strongly with her heritage and uses the term "Mexican American" most frequently to describe herself. She appreciates having the opportunity to label as Mexican American under the Hispanic-origin question on the census, but she states that she would prefer a Hispanic category on the race question: "I would like to have an option. I would put Mexican American." On the surface, Teresa's identification with whiteness might seem meaningless, as she says she would check Mexican American for her race if it were listed. However, when I went over the census form with respondents, I made it very clear that they could indicate a racial response of their choosing under "other race." Teresa knew that she had the option to write in "Mexican American" but chose not to do so.

Examining the narratives of Teresa and other respondents who said they would have checked "Hispanic" if available, I found that all but Ruben (see above) occupy a distinct position on the racial ideology continuum. These individuals believe racism is important in determining life chances today. However, they still turn away from racial politics and minimize personal experiences of discrimination. For example, while Teresa's activism primarily benefits Mexican immigrants and Mexican Americans, she does not attach a *racial* justice stance to her activism but rather views her work as "social justice." When asked about the term Chicano, she said:

No, [I would not use it,] because I see that term as being more radical. And I know that's a contradiction to what we just did there. [*Laughing, gesturing toward the building where she just led the meeting on workers' rights.*] But, that to me is brown power stuff, and to me that was more like a phase and not something that was permanent.

Teresa feels as though racial politics are outdated, but unlike those respondents in the "Leaving racism in the past" category, she does not believe that racial discrimination is primarily a problem of the past:

Teresa: I think that in general people, when they see a Hispanic vs. a white person that [they think] the white person is automatically going to be smarter, better looking, [a] harder worker than the Hispanic person.

JAD: Do you think you've ever been discriminated against? That people have thought that about you when they met you?

Teresa: It just happened a couple of months ago. I was at K-Mart, and some white gentleman, and I am sure he didn't mean anything by this, but he came up to me and he said, "Excuse me, *habla* uh . . . *habla inglés*, . . . [*mocking his Spanish pronunciation*]" and I turned around and said, "I have no idea what you just said. I am so sorry." And so he wanted to ask me what size of clothes I wore, because I was about his wife's size . . . and so I started talking clothing, and I told him about sizes. . . . and he said, "Thank you." And he walked away and he came right back and he said, "You know, I would have never thought that you could speak English so well. You can't even detect a Mexican accent on you. If I would have been blindfolded I would have thought you were white." I said, "Imagine that!" [*Laughing.*] So, yeah, no matter how hard they try to say there isn't [discrimination], there still is.

Teresa says that she is frequently mistaken for an immigrant, but she also notes that even when others know she was born in Del Rio, she feels she is still automatically assumed to be lower class and less industrious because she is Hispanic. While Teresa says these episodes happen often, she uses language throughout the interview to minimize these experiences. For example, in the story above, she calls the man a "gentleman" and excuses his behavior with, "I'm sure he didn't mean anything by this."

While these race-minimizing discursive frameworks and a disavowal of race-based organizing were common in both the categories of "Race is no barrier" and "Leaving racism in the past," respondents like Teresa differed in their emphasis on racism as a contemporary problem and more positive attitudes toward affirmative action. Teresa said that she has benefited from such programs:

Yes, and rightfully so, I think. When I went to college I won a migrant scholarship because I was a migrant, because most of the migrants are either black or Hispanic. So I got my first year of college paid for and then after that I had an athletic scholarship. Yeah, there're a lot of programs out there that help minorities. And we should be taking full advantage of those, I believe.

Teresa supports affirmative action programs, but she said she would not join an organization based on her race. She feels people should focus more broadly on justice issues, without drawing attention to racial difference.

Tom Reyes, a sixty-year-old school administrator in McAllen, feels similarly. Tom is from a middle-class background, college educated, and a fourth-generation Mexican American. Like Teresa, Tom identifies strongly with his Mexican heritage, speaks Spanish fluently, and is very active in his church, charities, and other social and civic groups. He uses the word "Hispanic" most often to describe himself but checked "white" on the census, "only 'cause there was nothing else. I didn't fit anywhere else." Tom says he would identify as "Hispanic" if it were listed as a race, as it reflects both his cultural heritage and the way others classify him. However, he did not feel strongly either way about the inclusion of a Hispanic racial option: "Sure, they can do that, but only if they feel it is necessary." Tom does support affirmative action and acknowledges that discrimination is a problem and something he faces personally. Yet he believes that every group has experienced it, explaining:

> Yeah, I think everybody has been [discriminated against], regardless of who they are. I've seen Germans discriminate against Jews, and I see Jews discriminate against others. Doesn't make a difference what ethnic background you are, you're gonna experience it one way or another.

Tom naturalizes discrimination, arguing that it is simply a part of life. This kind of "that is just the way it is" naturalization frame has been found among white European Americans (Bonilla-Silva 2010). The key difference, though, is that he is the one to whom prejudice is directed. For many respondents like Tom, discrimination is such a common occurrence that it has become unremarkable. A lifetime of experiencing what Essed (1991) has termed "everyday racism" can lead people of color to adopt a variety of coping strategies. Like the majority of Mexican Americans on the "white" side of the continuum, Tom chooses to deal with racism by minimizing these experiences.

Tom further does this by comparing Mexican Americans to Germans and Jews, both of whom he terms "ethnic" groups. Mary Waters (1990) found that her middle-class European American respondents often made no distinction between their experiences with their ethnic identities as Irish or German Americans and those of African Americans or Latinos. They argued that because they did not advertise their ethnicity, why should an African American or Latino? Waters finds this comparison problematic because of the blurred line that occurs between their "situational ethnicity" and the realities of racialized identities in the United States that actually have social costs (Waters 1990). One might think that Tom, who has experienced these social costs first hand, would align himself with other racialized groups such as African Americans. However, when he invokes a comparison to European Americans, he blurs the cost of racism at his own expense. As well, both Tom and Teresa spoke of racism as a phase that one passes through on the way toward acceptance as American. This further emphasizes their desire to align themselves with European Americans, who were eventually able to achieve acceptance as white Americans.

As with those in other positions on the continuum, the history of the legal whiteness of Mexicans also contributed to identification as white for those using the "Race/racism is transient" framework. Eddie Martinez, introduced in Chapter One, is an educator in his sixties in Del Rio. He grew up on the Mexican side of town in the barrio of San Felipe, the son of migrant workers. Recall that Eddie identified as "white," citing the segregation court case in Del Rio in which Mexican Americans fought to desegregate the schools by arguing that they were white. He noted that they were indeed legally defined as white, although it did not stop the segregation. Eddie said he would follow the law and check "white" but that it does not change who he is: "I'm still a Mexican."

Eddie has a long history of community involvement in Del Rio and was active in race-based organizing when he was younger. He said:

> I was a member of La Raza Unida party and supported their philosophy. I joined the marches. It was the sixties. We tried to send a message that there was no justice for the Mexican American in this part of the country. At that time we were second-class citizens.

Unlike respondents in the previous section, however, Eddie does not believe that racism is a part of only our past. He believes there is a lot of discrimination, particularly directed at immigrants, and he supports immigration reform. He is, however, no longer active in race-based organizing, explaining that things have changed and that type of rhetoric simply is not used anymore.

Frank Rodríguez is a construction worker in his early twenties in McAllen who also argued that while racism exists today, the rhetoric of racial difference is outdated. Frank is third-generation Mexican American and has a dark-brown complexion. Like Ruben, Frank identified as "white" on the census, stating that he has always been taught to put "white" when there is no "Hispanic" racial option. However, he says that he believes there should be a racial category for Hispanics because "I think we are big enough to be our own race, especially now that we are growing." Frank believes he has faced discrimination from others, both directly and indirectly. He has been mistaken for an immigrant, and he has also overheard whites talking negatively about people speaking Spanish. "They say this is America and people should speak English, but I think people should learn both languages," he said. Frank also feels that in the Rio Grande Valley, being Mexican American has its advantages. He told the story of a Mexican American sales clerk who gave him a discount because he is Hispanic. Frank thinks that discrimination can go both ways and that the way to combat it is to teach people that race does not matter.

Overall, the twelve individuals in this position on the racial ideology continuum speak of racial discrimination as a contemporary issue, but they still minimize and naturalize racism. Several express an understanding that racism is simply a phase we are going through, and none are comfortable organizing based on race. However, as they acknowledge racism in the present, they are much more supportive of programs to elevate the status of racial and ethnic minorities.

Conclusion

By introducing the racial ideology continuum and its relationship to identification with whiteness on the census, I have demonstrated the critical influence of color-blind rhetoric on the racial self-labeling of Mexican Americans. These findings both engage the current literature and break new ground. To date, the most common interpretation of Latino whiteness on the census is that it reflects lighter skin color, cultural assimilation, integration into the dominant majority, or a combination of these factors. Sociologist George Yancey best embodies this position in that he asserts that Latinos are well on their way to acceptance as white based on their self-reported racial identification as "white" on the census and their support of color-blind racial ideology (Yancey 2003). In other words, he argues that both claims to whiteness and color-blind rhetoric hold the same meaning for Latinos as they do for European Americans, that of integration and assimilation.

The narratives of my respondents challenge this argument on multiple levels. First, self-identified "white" Mexican Americans report that others do not perceive them as white. Indeed, only three of twenty-eight "white" Mexican Americans in the study note that persons ever identify them as racially white. Second, the overwhelming majority describe incidents of discrimination. While many refuse to attach the word "racism" to these episodes and do not wish to identify as racial minorities, they are still in fact experiencing racism. My results clearly indicate that identifying as "white" on the census is not an indication that Mexican Americans in these locales are gaining acceptance as racially white, nor is it a reflection of lighter skin color or cultural assimilation. Rather, it is a defensive strategy used to combat discrimination. Mexican Americans in all three sites use whiteness to assert their American citizenship and identity, defending themselves against presumptions that they are immigrants.

Proximity to the border has been linked to heightened incidents of racial profiling for Mexican Americans (Goldsmith et al. 2009). For respondents living in the border communities of Del Rio and Mission/McAllen, such episodes contribute to a desire to project an "American" identity. While Mexican Americans in the Dallas/Fort Worth area similarly respond in this way, claiming a white identity also serves to distinguish them from a sizeable African American population by expressing their desire not to be considered a comparable "racial" minority.

This strategic use of whiteness has a lengthy history in Mexican American communities (Foley 1998; Gómez 2007), but it is also infused with contemporary color-blind ideology (Gallagher 2003; Bonilla-Silva 2010). However, I find that the color-blind rhetoric espoused by my respondents differs substantially from that of European Americans in both form and function. My respondents do not claim not to "see" race; rather, they downplay racial divisions to deflect and deter racism directed at them. They are well aware of color and discrimination, but they feel that drawing attention to racial differences exacerbates the stigma attached to these identities. Instead, they choose to minimize experiences with discrimination and claim whiteness in hopes of finding greater acceptance.

Unfortunately, this strategy has not been successful: respondents from both higher and lower socioeconomic backgrounds still experience racial profiling and discrimination. My findings corroborate studies that have demonstrated the persistence of racialization in the lives of Mexican Americans and other Latinos (O'Brien 2008; Telles and Ortiz 2008; Vasquez 2011) and expose how experiences with racialization not only produce sentiments of racial "otherness" but also propel some to align themselves with whiteness. The next chapter focuses on how experiences with prejudice further inform the racial labeling choices of Mexican Americans who adopt a different strategy: those who identify outside the bounds of whiteness.

CHAPTER 3

"We were never white": Mexican Americans Identifying Outside the Bounds of Whiteness

Where is "Mexican"? I don't know what to write? We Mexicans were never white. Later they tried to call us white, but we were never white. I would write Mexican. . . . I don't know who made the question that way—probably some gringo who graduated college pero *[but] he does not know what it's like down here.*

MANUEL "MEME" RIVERA, MISSION, TX

Manuel "Meme" Rivera, a retired farmer in his seventies, sums up the confusion felt by many Mexican Americans as they approached the census questions for race and Hispanic origin. Meme wonders why "Mexican" is not listed as a racial option. By choosing to write it in himself, he articulates a boundary between Mexicans and whites that is based on how others have labeled and treated him. Meme further expresses pride in his Mexican heritage, saying, "We've been called so many things, and to me it doesn't matter what they call me. I am what I am, and that's what I'm going to be." Thus, his identification as "Mexican" is both a reflection of racialization by others as nonwhite and a self-asserted group identity that reflects pride in his cultural heritage. Meme's words reveal an understanding of how class, race, and region all inform how one sees racial divisions. While he has very little formal education, Meme feels he knows more about what it means to be a "Mexican" in South Texas than any educated outsider.

Just as Latino whiteness on the census has generally been read as a sign of lighter skin color and assimilation, "other race" responses like Meme's have been viewed as signifying less cultural or structural assimilation and darker skin color (Denton and Massey 1989; Yancey 2003; Tafoya 2004). However, Clara Rodríguez's (2000) groundbreaking investigation of "other race" responses among Latinos in New York challenges these interpretations, arguing that Latinos have a different perspective on the meaning of race. As alluded to earlier, drawing on an interview sample composed primarily of Dominicans, Puerto Ricans, and Ecuadorians, she asserts that Latinos understand race as a "cultural and/or political concept," different from the biological way in which race is constructed in the United States. Rodríguez argues that many Latinos see race in terms of cultural or national origin, but she also emphasizes that many other variables inform Latino racial identities. She writes: "Forces such as socioeconomic class, phenotype, family, the United States' racial structure, and experiences in schools, jobs, and social settings also are important determinants of racial identity" (Rodríguez 2000: 61).

Similarly, I find that assertions of racial "otherness" are the product of a number of intersecting factors. Specifically, Mexican American respondents' "cultural" responses to the race question are often inextricably linked to an American experience of racialization, in that they frequently serve as a strategic response to discrimination through the use of what Feagin (2010) has termed "home-culture frames." Feagin argues that many Latinos, particularly Mexican Americans who are often only a generation or two away from the immigrant experience, make use of home-culture frames, resisting assimilation into the dominant majority by choosing to maintain Latino cultural values and practices. He explains (2010: 189), ". . . the home-cultures can provide an important base for a quiet struggle against white cultural dominance and, often but not always, for some to mount a more aggressive anti-racist counter-framing against white oppression."

In Chapter Two, this "quiet struggle" can be found in the self-identified "white" Mexican Americans who hold tight to their Mexican culture. Yet, the white racial frame is ultimately the stronger influence on racial identification for this group. Most "other race" respondents, by contrast, use a race-based, home-culture counter-frame to assert racial difference from the dominant majority. This is exemplified in Meme Rivera's response to experiences of differential treatment: "I am what I am, and that's what I'm going to be." Meme's expression of pride in the face of prejudice represents a common theme among my interviewees.

Thus, what distinguishes "other race" Mexican American respondents from those who identify as "white" on the census is not greater attachment to their Mexican heritage, lower socioeconomic status, darker skin color, or more experiences with exclusion and differential treatment, as some have hypothesized. Rather, it is how they see racism and the strategies they employ to deal with discrimination that separate the two groups. In some cases, the development of these home-culture counter-frames leads to anti-racist activism. However, as with the espousal of color-blind ideology, the degree to which my respondents express anti-racist politics varies. As Feagin (2010) notes, many people of color are "multiframers" who reflect aspects of both the powerful white racial frame and competing anti-racist counter-frames. Thus, while identifying as racial "others," many Mexican Americans in the study continue to express aspects of color-blind ideology, the results of which are represented in the racial ideology continuum (Chapter Two, Figure 2.1). Chapter Three focuses on the "other race" continuum points: Racism is minimal, Racism is significant, and Racism is endemic.

Overall, of the thirty-seven Mexican American respondents who identify as "other race," twenty-one are in the "Racism is minimal" category. These individuals identify as racial "others" but still adhere to some aspects of color-blind ideology, including especially the minimization of racism (Bonilla-Silva 2010). Similar to those who labeled as "white," the overwhelming majority of these persons reported incidents of discrimination and then downplayed such episodes. At the next position on the continuum, eleven respondents in the "Racism is significant" group do not minimize racism but also do not espouse strong anti-racist rhetoric. Finally, the five interviewees in the "Racism is endemic" position are highly politicized about race, often aligning themselves with immigrants and African Americans in the struggle to fight racism.

All those who identified as "other race" had the opportunity to write in their own racial label on the census, and throughout the discussion I will refer to these terms. The overwhelming majority, thirty-one of the thirty-seven "other race" Mexican Americans, wrote "Hispanic" (twenty) or "Mexican American" (eleven) for their race; the remaining identified formally as "Mexican" (two) or "Chicana" (one).[1] Additionally, three wrote in responses indicating their American citizenship (e.g., "American," "U.S.-born"). In my interviews, it became clear that most use the terms "Hispanic" and "Mexican American" synonymously, often explicitly defining "Hispanic" to mean a person of Mexican descent. This regional understanding of Hispanic as only Mexican origin is likely due to the low percentage of non-Mexican Latinos in most areas of Texas, something that is well documented by other Texas-based research (Mindiola et al. 2002; Newby and Dowling 2007; Dowling and Newby 2010).

In Chapter Five I present detailed analysis of these labels, including how their usage varies based on context for both Mexican Americans and immigrants. However, in terms of formal identification on the census, Mexican American respondents' use of "Hispanic" versus "Mexican American" did not correspond to differing racial ideologies, such as embracing panethnic alliances or anti-racist politics. Though, in line with the link between assertions of "American" identity and color-blind ideology, the three respondents who identified racially as "Americans" are in the "Racism is minimal" position on the continuum.

Racism Is Minimal: "I stay on my side of town. Why go looking for trouble?"

Diana Espinosa is the daughter of a Mexican immigrant mother and a third-generation Mexican American father. She grew up in a *colonia* on the outskirts of McAllen. Throughout her youth, she and her family would migrate north seasonally to pick crops in other states. Now in her thirties, Diana works as a nurse in McAllen. When asked what she would answer for her race, she said, "I would check 'other' and write in 'American.'" While Diana says "Hispanic" is the term she uses most frequently to describe herself, her write-in response reflects her desire for others to see her as simply "American." Diana has a dark-brown complexion and notes that she is frequently assumed to be a Spanish speaker. She is fluent in Spanish and is happy to help when a Mexican immigrant needs assistance, but she wishes Anglos did not assume she speaks *only* Spanish. Despite acknowledging her frustrations with such situations, when I asked if she had ever been discriminated against or treated differently because of her racial or ethnic background, she replied that she had not. Diana does acknowledge that racism is present in contemporary society, but she minimizes her own experiences with racial profiling.

Her response is reminiscent of the Mexican Americans in Chapter Two who were often emphatic about having their American identities recognized and frequently minimized their experiences with racism. However, unlike those respondents, Diana does not use whiteness as a means of asserting her American identity. While Diana does not feel identifying as "white" is an option for her, she also does not want to separate herself from other "Americans" by claiming a "racial" identity as Hispanic. Her identification as racially "American" represents a creative solution to her predicament.

People in the "Racism is minimal" position on the racial ideology continuum see themselves as racially nonwhite and yet still espouse some elements of color-blind ideology (Bonilla-Silva 2010). However, Diana and two other respondents who answered similarly are the only "other race" Mexican Americans who did not indicate a Hispanic identifier for their race. Most Mexican Americans on the "other race" side of the racial ideology continuum responded more like Meme Rivera, quoted above, asserting pride in their heritage as a response to differential treatment.

Luisa Aguilar, a school administrator in her midfifties who lives in Mission, best exemplifies this dialectical process in her response to the race question:

I put "white" in 1990. There was no "Hispanic." In 2000, I checked "other" and wrote in "Hispanic." There was a big change from the year 1990 to the year 2000. I don't know, I just felt like I really needed to express the fact that I was Hispanic and not white. So that's the reason I did it. My views as to my ethnicity changed in those ten years. I'm more proud to be Hispanic now than I was back then. Because of the upbringing we had, segregation, racial discrimination, we were too embarrassed back then to say we were [Hispanic]. But I think as I've gotten older, I feel like the Lord put me in this race, and I should be proud of what I am. I mean I don't have anything to be embarrassed about. I think, so well, I am Hispanic. I do have different bloods, but none of us are pure this or pure that. So that's what I am. I am Hispanic.

Luisa spoke at length about both residential segregation and the harsh corporal punishment students would receive from Anglo teachers for speaking Spanish. Her comments show very specifically how her racial identity shifted as she overcame the internalized shame of discrimination. Over the course of ten years, her response to racism changed from that of claiming whiteness to expressing cultural pride in her heritage, a clear indication of exactly how racial ideology plays a critical role in the process of racial self-identification. Luisa's assertion that "none of us are pure this or pure that" also critiques the dominant white culture's insistence on exclusive and fixed racial categories. Emphasizing her "different bloods," Luisa continued:

Hispanic is someone who has a mixture of bloods, either Spanish, Italian, French, Mexican. And I have a little bit of all of those. My ancestors came from Spain, and some of them were blonde, blue eyed. And I have a lot of relatives that came from Mexico that looked very Indian, dark skin, the dark eyes. So I'm a little mixture of all.

Luisa's parents, both from Mexico, have a diverse ancestry that includes European and Indian heritage. This background is well understood within the Mexican national discourse that sees its citizenry as "mestizo," or a mixture of Spanish and indigenous cultures (Doremus 2001). However, Luisa does not identify racially as "Hispanic" simply because she relies on a "Mexican" definition of race versus an "American" one. Rather, her racial choice reflects an ideological response to discrimination encountered in the United States. Thus, her identity is the result of an interaction between her experiences with racialization and the strategic development of a home-culture frame to combat the stigma attached to her background.

Yet, while Luisa asserts this counter-frame, she also minimizes her experiences with racism. When describing Mission's history of rigid segregation, Luisa said:

> Most of the Hispanics or Mexican Americans, we lived on the south side of the railroad tracks. The north side was considered the Anglo side or the white side. So we hardly ever came across in the fifties over to this side even though the town, the businesses were on the north side. However, on the south side of town we had little groceries stores, meat markets. That's where we did our business, so we never experienced the discrimination then. But, we were told, "Don't go across to the north side. You have to stay over here."

Luisa's comments reveal how everyday racism becomes so naturalized that it is unremarkable (Essed 1991). Hence, despite knowing there was a whole side of town that she was not allowed to visit, she states that she "never experienced discrimination."

Similar to respondents who identify as "white," Luisa primarily thinks of discrimination in terms of individual bigoted acts, as opposed to the systematic racism of segregation and punitive policies. When asked directly if she had ever experienced discrimination, we had the following exchange:

> Luisa: No, I've never experienced it. But I've heard about others that have, and it goes back to the skin color. The darker you are the more they assume that that's what you are. I mean I'm not boasting that I look Anglo or anything like that. But I've never experienced it.
>
> JAD: Well, next I want to ask . . .
>
> Luisa: Yeah, wait.

JAD: OK, you want to go back to the discrimination question?

Luisa: Yeah . . . after I think about it. I need to tell a little story about a high school counselor that we had. He was the only counselor we had back in the sixties. I had never gone to see him, but when we were seniors, in the beginning of our senior year, and we were talking about what careers we wanted after high school . . . And he used to tell most of us that we were not college material, that we needed to go to a vocational school and so that to me is a form of discrimination because he was Hispanic himself and looked upon us like we were not worth anything else. At that time, we never did question or argue or anything like that. We just kinda went with it. "OK, that's what you think we need to do, we'll do it." Very few of the Hispanic kids back then were really college material in his eyes . . . and yeah, that was a form of discrimination, now that I think about it. And anyway, I went ahead and followed his advice of not going to college, so I went to beauty school, and finished in nine months with a little scholarship that they gave me. And I went and worked in a beauty salon for nine or ten years. . . . Finally, one day I said, "I don't like what I'm doing anymore. I should try going to college." I don't know why I listened to the counselor at that time. I'm going to try going to college and see if I can do it. So I was still doing beauty work and then I started college with maybe taking two classes at that time. I got A's in both of them, and I said, "Hey, I kinda like this. I'm going to keep enrolling, have some more classes and still continue working." I was very energetic at that time, so I would work all day long and my poor children, they didn't see me 'cause I would go to school at night.

Luisa finished her bachelor's and even went on to get her master's degree. Clearly, being told she was not college material represented a pivotal moment in her life. Yet, it is an exchange that she only now begins to process as discrimination. Perhaps because her counselor was a fellow Mexican American, it was more difficult for Luisa to recognize his behavior as "discrimination," which is often thought of as being perpetrated by someone of a racial background different from one's own. Nevertheless, her singling out of this incident, a one-on-one exchange with a guidance counselor, and not the pervasive segregation she described earlier in the interview, is also very telling. She searches her memory for acts perpetrated against her individually rather than discriminatory practices directed toward her larger Mexican American community, such as being forced to stay on one side of town.

Meme Rivera, discussed earlier, who identified as "Mexican" for his race, immediately spoke of differential treatment in his response to the census race question. Yet, when asked if he had ever faced discrimination, he responded similarly to Luisa: "I might not have been discriminated against because I knew where to go and where not to go. If I knew that I would make trouble in this and that, I don't need them. I go somewhere else." Meme also says that he never experienced discrimination because he knew to stay on his side of town. Both of Meme's parents were immigrants, and Meme struggled to learn English in school. Moreover, like Luisa, he remembers how the teachers forbade the use of Spanish, charging them a nickel for every Spanish word spoken, even during recess.

Thus, while acknowledging such practices as a form of discrimination, respondents in the "Racism is minimal" category often do not cite segregation and anti-Spanish policies when asked about their experiences with discrimination. This was true of younger individuals as well, who faced less rigid but still significant forms of language prohibition. Cristina Garza, a bilingual educator in her twenties in Del Rio, falls into this category. Her mother, a second-generation Mexican American, also worked in education, and her father, whose family dates back several generations in Texas, worked a low-wage job in sales. Cristina grew up on the Mexican side of Del Rio, in the barrio of San Felipe. While the segregation and rigid discrimination practices that several respondents discussed were no longer present during Cristina's youth, she feels that the Spanish language is still viewed as a hindrance. She felt pressure from her teachers growing up to speak only English, and as a result, she struggled to regain her Spanish:

> My first language is Spanish because my grandparents, my maternal grandparents, I guess you can say that they raised me because my parents were workaholics. And that's all they knew was Spanish. . . . And then I kinda lost it. It's not as polished as I would like for it to be. But now, being in a bilingual classroom, I think I've gained a little bit of it there. [I'm] not as fluent as I was before, but I would consider myself bilingual.

Cristina spoke of the enhanced pride she feels in recapturing her first language, which contributed to her decision to write in "Mexican American" for her race on the census. As a bilingual educator, she hopes to help students understand that speaking two languages is an asset. Additionally, Cristina is passionate about making sure her own children, when she has them, understand that one does not have to lose one's home culture to succeed, that maintaining Spanish fluency and getting an education are not mutually exclusive. She explains:

> I know for sure I would like for them to be exposed to the Spanish language. I think that's very important, especially now that we are moving to a global economy where you have to . . . it's important to learn other languages other than English. Of course, Spanish language and English and . . . [I would like for them to get an] education 'cause I know that's—it has gotten me out of sticky situations. I am able to pursue better careers.

Cristina feels that her college degree has allowed her to move up and helped her to defend herself. She does not have to tolerate the disrespect that many low-wage workers suffer, as having a degree means she "always has options."

Similar to Meme and Luisa, Cristina uses a home-culture counter-frame to assert pride in her heritage, specifically using Spanish as a tool against discrimination. Also, like other respondents in the category of "Racism is minimal," when asked about her personal experiences with differential treatment, she does not report the systemic practices that affected her. When I asked Cristina if she had ever experienced discrimination, our conversation went as follows:

> Cristina: Yes. It's sad to say 'cause I experienced it. 'Cause I am also working on my special education certification, and this was in San Marcos, and I never thought . . . I'd heard about, you know, racial issues and stuff, but it's totally different when you actually experience it yourself. And it is not a very good feeling, and [I] experienced it in San Marcos last summer.

> JAD: What happened?

> Cristina: Ah, at this [class] . . . we were taking a break, and I was the only, of course, Mexican there. All the other people were white. . . . There was a parent who came to . . . I guess tell the people that were going to be training like myself, you know, that the organization was good, the program was good, and you know, just kinda show us the positive side of it because her son had gone through the program. So this lady that says she was very, very educated, she introduced her son to everybody and we were kinda like in a semicircle on the steps and she went one by one. And then she got to me and she literally skipped me and introduced every-

body else and walked off. It's not to say . . . you can't say that I wasn't part of the circle because I was right there, but she just totally skipped me. And then I guess the other ladies noticed. And I didn't pay too much attention. I wasn't going to stoop to her level or anything like that. One of the ladies saw it and just kinda made sure that I was OK, that my feelings weren't hurt, and I was like, "No, don't worry about it." Well, on my next break, one of the ladies that was in the group said, you know so and so, you forgot to meet her. She comes all the way from Del Rio just to learn about this program so that way she can expand the teachings of this. And she kinda just smirked and walked off. But I never had to encounter her since then, and I don't know what I would do. Not so much what I would do, but I don't know how she would react because of the fact that I continued with the program. That was the only time I've ever experienced a racial discrimination.

Cristina chose her career path in large part because of linguistic prejudice she faced, and yet anti-Spanish sentiments are not mentioned here. Furthermore, even within this powerful episode of racism she cites, Cristina chose to ignore the perpetrator's behavior and told others not to worry about it.

Antonio "Tony" Diaz shares Cristina's strategy of minimizing racism. Tony is a probation officer in his twenties in the Dallas/Fort Worth area. When I asked Tony whether he has experienced discrimination, he replied:

I think I have. I mean, I'm never really sure because I don't talk about this. You can tell me something, and I just kind of, it just rolls off of me. I don't take things too seriously. Even if people say stuff to me and, um, I think I have been. Even when I think about it now, probably it was back in college, you know, dealing with financial aid and stuff 'cause the way we were talked to by certain counselors and stuff when dealing with financial issues and getting scholarships and stuff like that. Even, like the Hispanic tours at our school . . . [Then] the attention to all-white fraternity groups, and all-white groups or something like that, and so um, and you know it's little stuff like that . . . but I think during my college years, that's when I realized all this stuff, but it never really bothered me 'cause it was just like, "I can't change everybody's minds." So, I kind of let it roll off. It isn't until later on that I realize, "Oh, there's still discrimination."

Tony is the son of Mexican immigrants who worked in nearby factories. He was raised in a largely Mexican neighborhood and was held back in school to learn English, but he says that while growing up, he never saw discrimination. In college, however, he began to notice and identify certain behaviors as racially biased. For example, his college provided tours of the university specifically geared toward Mexican American students, which might have been a positive step toward inclusion. Instead, the tour guides often made comments that belied prejudice, sometimes in an insulting tone. Tony says that at the time, this did not bother him, as he was just grateful to have the opportunity to tour the campus and receive the information he needed to apply for financial assistance. After seeing how much better white students were treated, he reevaluated. However, while he labels these incidents discrimination, his attitude toward them is nonchalant. They are just "little stuff" that he lets "roll off" him.

While Tony wrote in "Mexican American" for his race and expressed a great deal of pride in his heritage, he feels his college degree and profession where he "polices" the behavior of others sometimes puts him at odds with his community. He explains:

> Tony: Just because I was raised here and the way I dress, the car that I drive . . . and, you know, I even got called a racist once because I was trying to bust this guy back at work. He's an illegal immigrant, and he committed so many violations. . . . [Then] I got called a racist and I'm like, "Get over it!" The first time I was called a racist. Well, basically I just filed a motion on him, judicial warrant, because he didn't, I mean he was basically still drinking, using drugs, stuff like that, so I just kinda did what I had to do.
>
> JAD: How did you respond when he called you a racist?
>
> Tony: I was just shocked. I was like, "What? I've never been called that before." I mean, it was just his opinion . . . but, he was like, "You need to help out your own people." I'm like, "I don't need to break the law to do that!" . . . Yeah, and I guess sometimes people feel like, you cannot achieve or we're not supposed to achieve to a certain level and stuff. It's kind of—be down with the family and, you know, have kids, take care of kids. But, my parents always put, I mean, I think they have a different mentality than Mexican people down in Mexico have. Here, we're about picking yourself up, you know, and they always told me, "Be better than that. Be better, have more money than them. Be better."

Tony describes the man with whom he had this confrontation as an "illegal immigrant." Rather than using terms such as "undocumented" or "unauthorized," he uses a word considered by many to be criminalizing and demeaning to immigrants (Inda 2006; Nevins 2010). No doubt his profession in law enforcement informs his word choice, but it also reflects a distancing maneuver. Tony makes a clear distinction between Mexicans in Mexico and those in the United States, thus distancing himself from Mexican immigrants in ways similar to "white" respondents.

Indeed, elements of Tony's story are reminiscent of those in the "Race is no barrier" category where respondents emphasized abstract liberalism in their assertions that hard work determines success. However, there are key differences in terms of racial ideology that place Tony in the "Racism is minimal" category. Those in the "Race is no barrier" position resist nonwhite racial labeling and espouse a strong color-blind ideology that includes discomfort with race-based funding for programs such as affirmative action. In contrast, Tony supports affirmative action and financial assistance for racial minorities, and he has been an active member in a number of race-based, albeit primarily social, organizations in high school and college. Moreover, when I spoke with Tony, he had recently been looking for books about Mexican American history. In his twenties, he has now come to recognize discrimination and wants to educate himself more about these issues.

Tony is also one of the lightest skinned respondents in the study. He says that while everyone in his neighborhood knows that he is Mexican American, strangers often assume he is white until they hear his name. But his ability to "pass," at least based on physical appearance, does not translate into racial identification as "white." This further highlights a key finding of the study, that my respondents' racial responses on the census are more closely tied to racial ideology and not necessarily a direct reflection of phenotype. Some of the lightest Mexican Americans selected "other race," and as explored in Chapter Two, several of the darkest interviewees identified as "white." This is not to say that skin color is irrelevant: external classification is crucial in shaping racial identification. I find, however, that the most influential factor determining how my respondents assert racial identities is how they choose to respond to racial "othering" through ideological frameworks that process, explain, and react to these experiences of racialization. Moreover, as Tony's story reveals, external classification is also based on surname, language, neighborhood, and other markers that, like phenotype, can create feelings of "racial" difference. Tony has never considered himself white despite his skin color. Moreover, his newfound ideological shift toward naming discrimination influences him to assert more strongly his feelings of cultural pride and even to seek out ways to educate himself about his heritage.

In sum, the twenty-one respondents in the "Racism is minimal" position on the continuum both employ home-culture counter-frames and adhere to some elements of color-blind ideology to varying degrees. All engage specifically in the color-blind frame of minimizing racism (Bonilla-Silva 2010), despite the discrimination (segregation, language prohibition, and racial profiling) that the overwhelming majority detailed at some point during the interview. Several further utilize tactics such as naturalizing discrimination, distancing themselves from immigrants, or both, but they typically exhibited far less of these discursive tactics than the "white" respondents in Chapter Two. Still, for these respondents, experiences with racism are often discussed as isolated incidents rather than a systemic or pervasive problem. Their primary coping strategies for dealing with such episodes when they occur is to avoid ("I stay on my side of town") or ignore ("I let it roll off me"). The next point on the continuum captures individuals who use similar coping methods but do not minimize the significance and impact of racism in their lives.

Racism Is Significant: "You can't fight the system, so you go with the flow"

Adrian Castillo is a business owner in his forties who lives in Mission, Texas. He grew up south of the railroad tracks on the Mexican side of town, the son of a second-generation Mexican American father and an immigrant mother. His father worked as a dishwasher, and Adrian never anticipated going to college. After high school, he began working and later started his own business. Despite his economic success, Adrian says he is often presumed to be lower class, an immigrant, or both due to his skin color:

> Adrian: So I think that they, you know, see you automatically and think, "I guess you're from Mexico." Especially down here 'cause we're so close to the border that we've had a lot of people from Mexico come shopping so I think they assume that if you're not white, you have to be from Mexico and they automatically talk to you in Spanish . . . unless it's somebody that you've known for a long time. I learned that they automatically label you and profile you, and say, "He's from Mexico."

JAD: How do you feel about that?

Adrian: It just depends. Sometimes, it gets kind of annoying . . . 'cause they're profiling me as soon as you walk into the store or you're gonna shop or whatever. So they automatically assume you're from Mexico. So it just depends . . . what it is, and of course what type of day you're having. Ugh, usually I start talking to them in English, and they switch gears and start talking to me in English. . . . If I would go to the same place wearing a suit and tie, or be more dressed up, then they treat you differently. . . . I think that's sad, . . . something that a lot of people do. They see more clothes and they say, okay, this person is, you know, up. I could go to a dealership and if I'm wearing shorts, they're not gonna pay too much attention to me 'cause they don't know me. If I go over to the same dealership, wearing a nice shirt and tie, oh, they're gonna treat me a lot more differently. You know, the same thing happens. Me, I'll notice those things and at the same time sometimes I think I don't wanna do business with them.

Adrian says that he faces this kind of profiling in part because he lives so close to the Mexican border, but he also notes that it has happened elsewhere during his travels both in and outside of Texas, including during a recent trip to New York. He says that he usually handles these incidents by speaking English, and he admits that he sometimes dresses more formally when going shopping for pricey items, so they "don't assume I can't pay for it." While he thinks about not doing business at some of these places, however, he neither confronts them nor walks out in protest. Rather, he attempts to ward off such incidents by dressing better and emphasizing English.

Adrian wrote in "Hispanic" for his race on the census, explaining that the term best reflects both who he is and how others classify him racially. Yet, while he speaks Spanish fluently, and passed the language onto his children, he does not feel invested in "drilling it into them" that they are Hispanic. Moreover, Adrian says he is certainly not interested in racial politics. He explained:

Well, I'm the type of person that will not join something if their center point is, "Join us 'cause I'm Hispanic." Well, they gotta do better than that. . . . Do this for you if your main selling point is 'cause you're Hispanic? You know I expect something better than that. Tell me, what's my benefits? What are the benefits for my company? What am I gonna get from this?

Adrian will not participate in a "Hispanic" organization unless he sees direct benefit for himself individually. Otherwise, he feels such efforts are a waste of his time. Adrian lives in a working-class Mexican American neighborhood and has primarily Mexican American social networks, which may lead him to feel less of a need to be vocal about his heritage with his children and in his activities. His cultural heritage is so much a part of his life that seeking out an organization that focuses on his Hispanic identity is of no import to him. But throughout the interview, Adrian's comments also reveal an acceptance that racist discrimination will continue and that there is little that can be done to either evade or combat such practices. Adrian and others like him occupy a unique position on the racial ideology continuum: they acknowledge that racism is significant, do not engage in race-minimizing discursive tactics, and yet also do not explicitly espouse an anti-racist agenda.

Orlando Calderon, a car salesman in his thirties who lives in the Dallas/Fort Worth area, shares Adrian's philosophy. Orlando acknowledges that racism is a part of his daily life, and he makes no efforts to minimize his experiences. He has a dark-brown complexion and feels he regularly encounters discrimination both when others assume him to be an immigrant and when it is obvious to others that he is from the United States. While he encounters such incidents, he nevertheless does not feel compelled to combat racism either on an individual level or through participating in political organizing. Rather, he argues, "You can't fight the system, so I go with the flow." Orlando has, however, volunteered his time teaching English to immigrants. He says:

> I think helping Mexicans from Mexico to establish [themselves] and helping them with further education and English . . . I actually worked a couple of times as a volunteer teaching English. [I would participate in] something like that, along those lines, helping people fill out applications, etc.

As a fourth-generation Mexican American, Orlando is far removed from the immigrant experience. He speaks Spanish but does not consider himself to be fluent. Growing up, his father worked at a service station, and his mother was employed part-time as a beautician. He and his family were the first Mexican Americans to move into the white working-class neighborhood where he was raised. Orlando acknowledges it was not always easy fitting in with either his white neighbors or Mexican Americans from the other side of town. But in junior high, his parents involved him in a Mexican folklore dance group. Orlando says that it was an amazing experience for him to learn about his culture and that it made him appreciate his heritage for the first time. It is something that he has carried with him ever since and that he feels helped him in developing a sense of pride in his identity.

Orlando wrote in "Hispanic" for his race on the census. He and his family now live in a working-class, predominantly Mexican and African American neighborhood. His wife is white, and their children, fifth-generation, multiracial Mexican Americans, speak little Spanish and have limited knowledge of their Mexican heritage. Orlando worries about how his children will "defend themselves" as they encounter prejudice. He says:

> I would like for them to acknowledge that they are of Mexican descent, and [that] they develop some sort of appreciation for it, and that they identify with it. . . . I've seen many a person that I know that are of Mexican descent, and they just totally deny it. And I think that's tragic. There was a person I know that was of Mexican descent, but pretended like he wasn't and [that he] didn't know any Spanish.

Orlando fears that his children could one day adopt such an attitude if he does not do more to instill a sense of cultural pride in them. His own identification as Hispanic and his efforts to teach his children to identify with their Mexican ancestry represent the use of a home-culture counter-frame, as he resists cultural assimilation and alliance with the dominant majority. This move is also a response to racialization, as he feels that no matter how culturally assimilated he or his brown-skinned children might become, it is unlikely they could ever be accepted as racially white. Thus, he believes having an understanding of their Mexican heritage could help his children to embrace this racial otherness, rather than internalize it as a stigmatized identity.

Both Orlando and Adrian fully acknowledge racism in their lives and the lives of others, but beyond cultural maintenance and the adoption of a home-culture counter-frame, neither utilizes strategies of working to combat racial discrimination either by directly confronting those who profile them or by engaging in political organizing. Rather, they seem to accept racial discrimination as a significant but inevitable component of daily life. They naturalize racism, although in a way quite different from European Americans. Their remarks do not reflect a lack of concern regarding racism ("Oh well, that's just the way it is") or a perception of racism as a transient phase, such as those in Chapter Two maintained. Rather, they are deeply bothered by racial prejudice directed at them and others but feel powerless to change things.

Some respondents in this category also feel that they have seen a lot of change in race relations over the years, and this makes them feel less compelled to be involved now in organizing for racial justice. One such person is Sandra Alvarez, a third-generation Mexican American teacher in her fifties who lives in Del Rio. Sandra was once quite active in racial politics, but like Orlando and Adrian, now adopts a less confrontational approach. Sandra references her involvement in La Raza Unida political party:

> We went to different places, just to, you know, make people understand that we all have rights and that back then it [discrimination] was very strong. It's still strong now. I know it is, [but] I'm not as involved. I'm not involved anymore with it because I see that our rights have been met after Martin Luther King, so many things changed. And we got to see those changes, you know?

Sandra believes the kind of extreme prejudice that motivated her political involvement when she was younger is no longer a problem. She describes one example of such an episode that occurred when she and her husband moved to San Angelo, Texas, for a brief period while her husband was in college:

> And I was already, you know, grown-up, a mommy and everything. And we were looking for an apartment, you know, something my husband could afford 'cause he was going to college. So we found a little apartment, it was a garage apartment, real cute, and the guy got out—big, white guy. . . . And he showed us the little apartment. I loved it and went on and on . . . , and he says, "Well, I would love to rent to you all, but the neighbors would not accept your race in this neighborhood." And I went—and that was in sixty—I would say around sixty-nine, during my Chicano, my race—my brown berets—or whatever you wanna call 'em back then. So I was not intimidated. I was not because I did let him have it. My husband said, "Sandra, you didn't have to talk to him like that." "Oh, yes, I did because he insulted us"—not necessarily my race, he just insulted us as human beings.

Sandra tells a poignant story of an overt act of discrimination where she and her husband were denied housing because of their race. While Sandra acknowledges that racism is still quite common, she feels that the civil rights movement did a lot for Mexican Americans and hence feels less of a sense of urgency to be involved politically today.

Overall, the eleven respondents in the "Racism is significant" position on the continuum do not utilize elements of color-blind ideology such as minimizing their experiences with racial discrimination, but they also do not currently explicitly espouse anti-racist politics. They use home-culture counter-frames and cultural maintenance strategies to cope with racism, and their approach to specific racist encounters is usually less confrontational. For example, they might ignore such behavior or avoid going to a store where they have been racially profiled. The next section explores the narratives of those who take a stronger, more active stance in their adoption of anti-racist ideologies.

Racism Is Endemic: "We should work with blacks and immigrants, all of us together"

Jerry Velasquez is a police officer in his early thirties who lives in the Dallas/Fort Worth area. Jerry is the father of two young children and founder of a local program for disadvantaged youth. The program helps young men in low-income neighborhoods turn away from gang violence and toward competitive sports, learning important lessons about discipline, self-esteem, and teamwork along the way. Jerry explains:

> A lot of these kids are twelve, thirteen, fourteen, fifteen, even up to twenty years old gangbanging folk. They don't think that they're going to make it past sixteen. And I'll ask them, "Where do you see yourself in ten years?" "I didn't think I was gonna make it past ten years." OK, "Where do you see yourself next year?" "Well, if I make it, I'd . . ." and they tell me their goals and aspirations. . . . And so a lot of these kids I bust smoking marijuana. Instead of arresting them, and ruining their lives for a misdemeanor, I say, "I'll give you a Class C ticket. I'll make it disappear if you show up in my program." . . . And then I realize, looking back, I'm like this is where I came from. No one sees that now. But, I bring a picture [to show them that] I came from here. I came from where you came from, and look where I'm at now. I mean, I'm a cop. I'm not rich, but I'm happy. And I've got my kids and I've got this and this and this. They're like, "Wow, we can do that." So all I gotta do is push them.

Jerry has brought some of these young men onto the police force and credits a Mexican American police officer with helping him out of the violence of the streets and into this career path. He says: "I think that makes us better cops than most. So, we don't look at these people that live in low-income areas as dirt."

Growing up, Jerry had a negative image of the police, as they often racially profiled and harassed him. Even as an officer himself, he is sometimes pulled over by the police while off-duty. Just recently, a young white officer pulled Jerry over, demanding to see his license and registration. When Jerry attempted to warn him that he was an officer and his gun was in the vehicle, the man silenced him, "I said license and registration, Pancho!" The situation escalated, as unfortunately Jerry's proof of insurance was a few days past expiration. While he had renewed it, he did not have the new card with him. Jerry describes the scene:

And so he started pulling me out of the car! He's like, "You know I have to tow your vehicle. What do you think I should do?" And I was like, "Well, I think you should call and verify the insurance." He's like, "Where do you get off telling me what to do and blah blah blah." . . . Then he realized it. He's like, "Do you work anywhere?" I was like, "I tried to tell you that I'm a police officer and that I am armed and that the place where I got my wallet from is where I've got my handgun. And if I was a bad guy, you would have been shot by the way you were treating me." And so he freaked out. He's like, "Oh, my God." And I said, "So, I want the name and number of your supervisor and I'll be giving him a call." . . . And it turns out he only had joined the academy, not a lot of training, just like two months. But, that's happened to me several times. And I've been yanked out of my car window, pulled out, at gunpoint when I was eighteen years old . . . the way I dressed, they yank me out, handcuff me. I'm like, "What are you taking me in for?" [He said:] "You look like a robbery suspect, a robbery that just occurred at a 7-11." And then I hear on the radio the suspect's description and yeah, it's like my description, but the car is like a freakin' Honda and I was driving a Chevy. So, have I been discriminated against? Yeah, totally. I've been called a wetback, a piece of shit—even while in uniform! "I don't want you here. I want a white cop." So, yeah, it's a fact of life, it's gonna happen. . . . You get looked at—they give you that dirty look in places that you normally go to.

Jerry went on to describe a range of experiences with discrimination, including the poor service he receives at restaurants and stores and the tracking he encountered in his schooling. In high school, he was placed in the English as a Second Language (ESL) program even though he was raised by a third-generation Mexican American mother and spoke almost no Spanish at the time. He argued with the school, explaining that he spoke English, was a good student, and wanted to go to college. They moved him out of ESL, but he discovered too late that he was placed in the noncollege-bound track. Jerry says his personal history makes it easy for him to understand how young people from low-income backgrounds, particularly Latinos and other people of color, become discouraged. He responds to these incidents by trying to help young men of color learn to see their future possibilities.

Jerry occupies the most extreme end of the racial ideology continuum, believing that racism is endemic, a pervasive part of everyday life and something that must be combated. While Jerry does not see himself as the "political type," his community work is grounded in anti-racist politics. Jerry identifies as "Hispanic" on the census, and he expresses a great deal of pride in his Mexican heritage. This pride did not come easily for Jerry both because of the discrimination he faced from whites and because of abuse he received from Mexican American peers in his youth. The latter taunted and even beat him because of his inability to speak Spanish. He recalled their words, "What do you mean you don't speak Spanish? *Tienes un nopal en la frente* [You have a cactus on your forehead]," a common expression to describe someone who looks phenotypically Mexican. As a result of these experiences, Jerry became vigilant about learning Spanish, although not by taking classes. Instead, while in high school, he interacted with the immigrants in his community and served as a translator. His Spanish skills were then strengthened when he worked in construction for years after high school alongside mainly Mexican immigrants.

Jerry feels that his fluency gives him a greater sense of clarity and purpose about who he is. Reclaiming his heritage serves as a powerful home-culture counter-frame that is at the root of his community activism: In his program, he primarily assists low-income immigrant and U.S.-born Latino youth. Moreover, on a personal level, he is now attempting to teach his young children Spanish. Their mother, his ex-wife, is white, but they inherited his skin color, and Jerry fears that like him, they will struggle with acceptance from Mexican Americans if they do not learn the language.

Jerry's story also reveals the difficulties faced by multigenerational Mexican Americans who are clearly racialized as nonwhite and yet also experience exclusion from other Mexican Americans and Mexican immigrants for perceived cultural assimilation. This is a phenomenon well documented by research on the interaction between U.S.-born Mexican Americans and Mexican immigrants (Vila 2000; Ochoa 2004; García Bedolla 2005; Jiménez 2010), and yet it is a topic that has rarely been explored as a factor informing racial identification. The development of home-culture counter-frames for Jerry and others like him in the study involves actively working to gain greater cultural competency (Spanish-language skills, for example) in a strategic move to enhance acceptance from other Mexican Americans. This further demonstrates how the development of these home-culture counter-frames among my respondents is very much rooted in an American experience of racialization. Excluded by whites, Jerry turns to "home" cultural practices that were not a part of his own home growing up. His mother did not speak Spanish to him because she did not want him to face discrimination. Ironically, it is by learning the language that he finds acceptance and the vision to create a program that helps to empower others.

One of Beatriz "Bea" Fernandez's greatest regrets is not teaching her children Spanish. A third-generation Mexican American in her forties, she lives in Fort Worth where she works as a secretary. Bea is the daughter of migrant workers, and as a child, she struggled to learn English in school:

> It was very, very hard. I went into the first grade, which was all in English, and I did not speak a word of English and the teacher was white and did not speak any Spanish. . . . I remember how hard it was and how I would cry because I couldn't communicate, and they would get mad at you for speaking Spanish. . . . My kids, I didn't teach them [Spanish]. . . . I just didn't want my kids to have an accent. And now they need it. People go up to them talking in Spanish, and they just look over at me. And it is kind of embarrassing to me because they look Hispanic and like they should know [Spanish].

Like Jerry, her two teenage children now struggle with both discrimination from whites and tension in their interactions within the Mexican American community because of their inability to speak the language. Her children have taken Spanish classes at school, but they found the experiences frustrating, as textbook Spanish is not helping them to communicate. Bea would like to teach them herself, but she never learned to read or write in Spanish. She feels angry that she was made to feel so embarrassed by her Spanish so early in life.

Bea wrote in "Mexican American" for her race, emphasizing that this is her cultural identity and how she is classified by others. When I asked Bea about her experiences with discrimination, she immediately cited the linguistic issues she faced in her youth and also went on to discuss day-to-day experiences with discrimination that she encounters now, as others make assumptions about her based on her skin color:

> My husband and I went to buy a car. The owner, a white man, looked out at us and immediately sent over a Mexican American guy working there to talk to us. We think he just took one look at us and assumed that we didn't speak English. So yes, I think discrimination is there. I think it is everywhere. So yes, many times I have been discriminated against, and even by my own. I think that Mexican Americans are often discriminated against by Mexicans. They say, "Oh, you're from here."

Bea believes that discrimination is "everywhere" and that we should work to change things. While she finds herself too busy with work and parenting to actively participate in organizations aimed at fighting racial discrimination, she supports anti-racist efforts and would like to become more involved:

> Sometimes I wish I knew more about issues, like immigration, because even though it does not affect me or my kids, but really it does in a way. Because when people see me or my kids, they just see Mexicans. That is how the teachers see my children. I remember when my daughter came home one day and said she wanted to dye her hair, to lighten it. She was thirteen. And I told her she was too young and besides she has pretty hair. But she thought it would help with the discrimination. So if I could, I would be more involved in getting people not to discriminate.

Bea aligns herself politically with immigrants, in part because she recognizes that her family is regarded as simply "Mexican" by others. Bea further discussed a level of solidarity she feels with African Americans, who share this experience of racial discrimination. While growing up, she says, "if a girl dated a white or black guy, there was talk," but "marrying someone white was not as bad as black." Bea rejects this mentality, noting that both her children are dating African Americans. She and her husband, who is also Mexican American, are comfortable with their children's dating choices: "We just stress that he's got to be nice, clean-cut, and churchgoing, and that is all that matters to us."

Juliana Sanchez, introduced in Chapter One, is a retired teacher's assistant in her seventies who also lives in the Dallas/Fort Worth area. She grew up in a neighborhood composed of African Americans and Mexicans, where they lived "all poor, all together." Juliana gets very angry when Mexican Americans discriminate against African Americans. Like Jerry and Beatriz, she strongly feels that racism is pervasive and that Mexican Americans need to work with African Americans and Mexican immigrants to seek social change. "If it wasn't for *los negros* [the blacks], we would have nothing," she says. "They really helped to open a lot of doors for us." Juliana worked in bilingual education for many years and is especially sensitive about the plight of undocumented immigrants. While Juliana has a very light/olive skin tone, she says she would never identify as white. When filling out her census form, she wrote "Mexican," explaining, "I am very proud of my race." For Jerry, Beatriz, and Juliana, living in a racially diverse urban area with a significant African American presence made negotiating their status vis-à-vis this group an important component of their racial ideology.

For two other respondents in the "Racism is endemic" category who live in border communities, relations with African Americans figure far less prominently in their anti-racist politics. Given the demographics of these cities, they simply have little interaction with African Americans, and hence, they focused more specifically on the needs of Mexican Americans and Mexican immigrants. Marco Valdez, a third-generation Mexican American in his sixties who works as a nurse in Mission, spoke emphatically about the need for Hispanic people to work for social change:

> We [my wife and I] feel that we have to let people know exactly where we stand, what we think of certain things, the way the country is run. And you need to have that—people need to speak up instead of being guided by somebody else's purposes or needs or whatever they are. . . . And I think as Hispanics we don't always speak up as much as some of the other races. But I think we need to stand up and be noticed.

Marco's anti-racist activist roots stem from his early experiences with Jim Crow–style segregation in Texas. Specifically, he remembers two incidents that occurred following his return from serving in the army. Marco recalls:

> When I was in the army, I was coming back from Korea, and I was in the bus, my friend and I. For the bus stop, everybody got off at the same time. The line was very long, so we decided to go to a restaurant, and we

were told outright that they did not serve Mexicans, and that was in the 1960s. And the other time was when we went to a little town close to Corpus Christi. It's called Robstown. It was a country-western entertainment bar, and my friend and I, we had our dates and we were also refused there because they refused Mexicans at that time.

Being denied service at a restaurant right as he returned from serving his country had a particularly powerful impact on Marco. He was no longer willing to tolerate such forms of bigotry and felt that he deserved to be treated as unequivocally American. Unlike Mexican Americans in Chapter Two, however, "other race" respondents like Marco did not utilize claims of whiteness to assert their American identities. Instead, he became active politically in organizations that relied on a politics of racial difference, such as La Raza Unida political party. Moreover, while he acknowledges that things have changed, he still feels discrimination is a huge problem for Mexican Americans and Mexican immigrants, and he remains active in fighting injustice.

Del Rio resident Olivia Cuevas remembers when her father returned from serving in the military during World War II with a similar attitude. Termed the "G.I. Generation" (Camarillo 1971), Mexican American WW II veterans returned from fighting for their country to find they were still second-class citizens at home. It was veterans like Olivia's father who initiated the American G.I. Forum, a Mexican American civil rights organization that began in Texas in 1948, spreading across the Southwest, and challenging discrimination (Camarillo 1971; M. García 1989). Olivia, now in her early forties, speaks of her father's impact on her identity:

> He served in World War II and was very adamant about receiving the same privileges as everyone else because he served our country. So he came back from World War II full of pride saying, "I am a Mexican American." And he would tell us we were Mexican Americans. And I always identified with that until recently. Now just "Hispanic" seems more the term people use.

Olivia wrote in "Hispanic" for her race on the census because she feels it has become a more popular term. During the seventies when she was an adolescent, she identified as "Chicana" and attended political events with her older sister. Olivia is now a college graduate and dental assistant. Like Beatriz, she says working full-time, with two children, makes being active politically now a challenge. However, while the way she labels herself may have changed over time, her politics remain the same.

Olivia feels that the struggle for equality is certainly not over. She complains that she is often mistaken for an immigrant and that she receives poor service at stores, restaurants, and other businesses. Moreover, she notes she has faced discrimination on job interviews:

> I think that I have been in situations where it starts that way and then when they find out I speak English and then they change. That has happened at job interviews or going into a store to buy something. Sometimes I have just walked out. Especially when you are going to buy something really expensive, like when I was shopping for a car. I just walked out when they treated me that way. I want to deal with some place that will treat me equally.

Olivia's response here exemplifies the attitudes of those on this extreme end of the continuum. They do not minimize racism, and they are adamant about not tolerating discrimination from others. In sum, Mexican Americans in the "Racism is endemic" position view racism as pervasive and institutional, do not excuse or minimize racial discrimination, and espouse strong anti-racist politics. For all in this category, this means aligning themselves with Mexican immigrants, and for those in the Dallas/Fort Worth area, their politics extend to include African Americans.

Conclusion

Research has clearly demonstrated that Latinos, and Mexican Americans specifically, experience racialization differently, dependent upon a number of factors, including phenotype, gender, socioeconomic status, level of cultural assimilation, and generational status (Rodríguez 2000; Vasquez 2011). As previously discussed, some have suggested that racial labeling as "white" vs. "other race" on the census is a reflection of such divergent experiences within the Latino population, particularly that these racial responses reveal two very different groups in terms of their levels of assimilation and inclusion in U.S. society (Tafoya 2004). However, my interviews suggest that "other race" Mexican Americans in Texas do not differ substantially from those who identify as "white" in terms of skin color, cultural attachment, or experiences with racial discrimination.

What distinguishes "other race" Mexican Americans in the study is how they choose to respond to racialization. Rather than publicly adopting "white" identities, they develop home-culture counter-frames, accepting and at times even embracing their racial difference from the dominant white majority. The strategic element of the adoption of home-culture counter-frames for many respondents is perhaps most evident in stories like that of Jerry Velasquez, who deliberately sought to acquire greater cultural competence in his Mexican heritage in order to fashion a stronger sense of self-confidence and purpose in the face of daily encounters with racism. The stories of my respondents highlight the importance of external classification and the persistence of discrimination in shaping Mexican American racial identity, including how such experiences can even strengthen cultural resilience and foster a politics of racial difference.

Yet, while respondents like Jerry espouse a strong anti-racist ideological stance, not all "other race" Mexican Americans do so. Indeed, over half of "other race" Mexican Americans still engage in race-minimizing discursive tactics, and three-quarters of all Mexican Americans in the study utilize some aspects of color-blind ideology, albeit in ways quite different from European Americans. These results resonate with O'Brien's (2008) research on how Latinos and Asian Americans fashion their own racial ideologies that frequently differ from those of both whites and African Americans, reflecting their distinct experiences as part of the "racial middle."

The location of Mexican Americans in the U.S. racial order, however, is particularly unique when compared with African Americans, Asian Americans, and even other Latinos, in that their history includes a paradoxical position as legally white, yet socially nonwhite (Gómez 2007). This history includes Jim Crow–style segregation practices that existed alongside both legal whiteness and a perpetual association with foreignness. I argue that this complex legacy shapes the racial rhetoric of Mexican Americans today, as they define their experiences with differential treatment and assert racial identities. Fractured by strikingly different approaches to combating discrimination and their accompanying racial language, many Mexican Americans oscillate between understanding themselves as racial minorities and attempting to project white identities. Contemporary color-blind ideology further complicates their identity negotiations, as many have internalized an understanding that talking about racism is "un-American" (O'Brien 2008). While respondents in this chapter do not claim whiteness to assert their American identities, their identities are firmly rooted in an American understanding of race that is influenced by color-blind ideology. I believe this helps to explain why even many of those who self-identify as outside the bounds of whiteness still minimize their experiences with racism. The implications of the use of color-blind ideology among Mexican Americans will be discussed in detail in Chapter Six. The next chapter focuses on respondents socialized outside the United States, exploring how Mexican immigrants navigate racial labeling by drawing on both Mexican and American racial constructs.

CHAPTER 4

"In Mexico I was . . .": Translating
Racial Identities Across the Border

As we sat across the kitchen table, Maria Lopez thoughtfully looked over the racial options on the census form. "Well, what can I answer?" she asked in Spanish. Responses like Maria's were the most common that I received from Mexican immigrants. While Mexican Americans were often more firm in their racial choices, immigrants frequently asked what they could answer or what the "correct" answer was. After a long pause, Maria opted to write in "Hispanic" under the "other race" option, explaining that she had heard the label used to describe "people who speak Spanish here in the U.S." When I asked how she felt about the term she had chosen, she shrugged and said, "I am Mexicana, but the form belongs to the U.S. government and here we are Hispanics." Maria continued, explaining that she has always understood her "*raza*" in terms of her nationality as Mexicana, but she had never been asked to mark her race on paper before coming to the United States. While she still finds the common use of such questions peculiar, after eight years of living here, she has learned that "Hispanic" is her expected response. Maria feels the use of this label in the context of formal identification in the United States is only temporary for her, as she plans to leave her job as a housekeeper in Fort Worth to return to Mexico in just a few years.

As immigrants like Maria arrive in the United States, they often find themselves identified by others as "Hispanic" or "Latino," whether they feel any connection to these terms or not (Oboler 1995; Rodríguez 2000; Roth 2012). A conflict results between what Cornell and Hartmann (1997) term "asserted" or self-identification and "assigned" or imposed identification by others. In other words, Latino immigrants find that how they define themselves may not correspond with how they are classified, as the conceptions of race they bring with them from Latin America differ substantially from U.S. racial constructs (Rodríguez 2000).

Race in the United States has historically emphasized separate and distinct racial categories, with a particular focus on delineating who could be classified as white and thus eligible for citizenship and full civic participation (Omi and Winant 1994; Haney-Lopez 1996). Whiteness in the United States represents an elusive social identity category that has excluded not only African Americans but also Asians, Native Americans, and—most pertinent to this study—Latinos/Hispanics (Haney-Lopez 1996; Menchaca 2001; Foley 2006). A belief in white superiority and a fear of racial "miscegenation" led to the enactment of laws to prevent interracial marriage, protecting a conception of white racial purity. Indeed, laws of hypodescent dictated that just "one drop" of African ancestry was all that was needed to designate one as legally nonwhite (Davis 1991). These laws were enforced until they were ruled unconstitutional by the 1967 *Loving v. Virginia* U.S. Supreme Court decision (Pascoe 1991; Haney-Lopez 1996). Years later the legacy of such practices continues to shape how Americans think about racial classification in terms of discrete racial categories, rather than the multiple and overlapping identities that characterize many Latin American countries (Rodríguez 2000).

Racial Constructions in Mexico

While the dominant racial paradigm in the United States is predicated on notions of racial purity and exclusive racial categories, Mexico's national racial discourse is based on an understanding of Mexican people as "mestizos," a mixture of Spanish and indigenous ancestry (Doremus 2001; Deans-Smith and Katzew 2009; Sue 2013). This racial mixing, in fact, forms the foundation of the country's racial narrative. However, the historical and contemporary status of race relations in Mexico is neither free from racial hierarchies nor liberated from notions of European superiority (Deans-Smith and Katzew 2009; Sue 2013). The *casta* (caste) paintings, created in the eighteenth century, provide a fascinating glimpse into the construction of racial hierarchies in colonial Mexico. The paintings show an array of families, illustrating racial mixtures involving European, African, and Indian ancestry. The artwork testifies to the intricate caste system that characterized racial classification during this time period. In stark contrast to a U.S. emphasis on racial purity, these paintings openly acknowledged racial mixture. However, they are not to be interpreted as a sign of racial equity. William B. Taylor (2009: x) writes:

This was no rainbow coalition of cultural diversity two centuries before Jesse Jackson. On the contrary, *casta* paintings put people in their racialized place. . . . Like the early history of race in the United States, the *castas* validated white superiority in their own way. The mixing of races depicted in the paintings imagines a whitening process in which the Indian side of the family tree recedes, with descendants whitened, both racially and culturally. The paintings depict black and white mixture moving in the same, uplifting direction, but never quite getting there.

Thus, notions of racial mixture in colonial Mexico were deeply entrenched in an understanding of European superiority, in which indigenous and black Mexicans achieved a higher status through race mixing.

Shortly after Mexico achieved independence from Spain in 1821, a new law mandated that Mexican citizens would not be classified by race on government documents. The end of slavery in Mexico soon followed in 1829 (Deans-Smith and Katzew 2009). Deans-Smith and Katzew (2009: 12) write: "In theory, then, the Spanish monarch's 'subjects' were transformed in the nineteenth century into (ostensibly raceless) 'citizens,' equal before the law, able and willing to pursue their individual self-interests while redirecting their loyalties away from localities and toward the emerging (abstract) nation-state." The move away from racial demarcation signified a shift in the racial discourse in Mexico, from acknowledging blackness (and strands of Asian ancestry present in some parts of Mexico) toward a conception of Mexicans as Spanish and Indian. The development of the ideology of *mestizaje* formed, proclaiming mestizo identity as the crux of Mexico's national identity. Yet, despite the nineteenth century move away from a caste system toward an emphasis on a unified national racial identity, aspects of the colonial racial hierarchy remained. Spanish origin and lighter skin represented a higher-level status, and indigeneity and darker skin were still linked to a lower-class status. Moreover, the idea that whiteness is achievable through social mobility also remained (Dean-Smith and Katzew 2009; Taylor 2009).

The outcome of this discourse of *mestizaje* is a contemporary understanding of the term *"raza"* in Mexico as reflecting a sense of "peoplehood" linked to their nationality as Mexicans.[1] However, this construction of *raza* does not mean that Mexicans do not distinguish themselves based on class, phenotype, and membership in indigenous communities. Upper-class Mexicans may label themselves, or others may identify them, as *"güero,"* a term meaning white or light skinned, in reference to their higher social position, regardless of their actual skin color. Terms like *"güero"* and *"blanco"* are also used as color or phenotypic descriptors for those who are lighter skinned, while *"moreno"* and *"prieto"* describe darker skin. Historical and contemporary privilege tied to European origins means that lighter-skinned Mexicans are often found in elite positions throughout Mexico. While the dominant racial discourse describes all Mexicans as mestizos, numerous indigenous communities in Mexico identify themselves in terms of their specific Indian heritage. Some Mexicans may also identify with their roots as Afro-origin or Asian, but the mestizo racial narrative largely ignores the presence of these groups, making such identity claims less common.[2] Hence, the creation of the mestizo as a national identity effectively marginalizes groups such as indigenous and Afro-origin Mexicans who are left out of this construction (Doremus 2001; Dean-Smith and Katzew 2009; Sue 2013).

In terms of formal identification, Mexican federal documents such as the census do not ask for racial group membership, but rather whether one speaks an indigenous language or identifies oneself as a member of an indigenous community.[3] In contrast to a U.S. model of racial classification that has been historically dominated by hypodescent where individuals are assigned the racial identity of their nonwhite heritage, in Mexico it is not the biological presence of Indian ancestry that makes one indigenous. Because the majority of Mexicans are considered mestizos who have some Indian ancestry, being Indian means speaking an indigenous language or considering oneself part of such a community.

Thus, Mexican immigrants arrive in the United States with a fundamentally different understanding of race, one that is primarily synonymous with national origin or cultural membership rather than based on skin color. Maria's remarks above specifically highlight an important component of this process that is often not addressed: not only are U.S. racial identity categories foreign to new immigrants but so is the very act of affiliation with a "racial" group.[4] In the United States, identifying one's race is ubiquitous. Americans are routinely asked to indicate their racial group membership on paperwork for school, employment, housing, and medical care. However, this is not the case in Mexico.

Some scholars have argued that Mexico and other Latin American countries' relative disavowal of racial group identification signifies a type of color-blind ideology. Indeed, Eduardo Bonilla-Silva (2004) argues that racial classification and ideology in the United States is actually experiencing a "Latin Americanization" process whereby the racial discourse is shifting from a historical black-white binary classification system to a color- and class-based model that simultaneously uses a color-blind rhetoric to deny race and racism. This transition, Bonilla-Silva believes, parallels the development of such raceless rhetoric in many Latin American countries. He argues, however, that by creating a national discourse that denies or downplays racial difference and instead advances a singular racial identity ("We are all Mexican" or "We are all mestizos"), the very real inequalities that exist based on color and phenotype in countries such as Mexico and Brazil, for example, are minimized and ignored, making it more difficult to talk about discrimination (Bonilla-Silva et al. 2003; Bonilla-Silva 2004). Bonilla-Silva notes how a similar expression of "we are all American" has become a common trope of color-blind ideology in the United States, evoked by white Americans who minimize race and do not acknowledge that some groups are treated as more American than others (Bonilla-Silva et al. 2003).

However, the degree to which Latin American racial ideology resembles U.S.-style color-blind framing is a point of controversy among scholars. Bailey (2009) contends that at least in the context of Brazil, racial ideology is not the same as color-blind discourse in a U.S. context. He argues that Brazilians both "see" color and acknowledge discrimination. They simply do not affiliate color with membership in a racial group to the degree that persons in the United States do so. Sue (2013) finds similarly that Mexicans recognize skin color as a salient marker of social status despite Mexico's national discourse of racial unity. Hence, Bailey (2009) and Sue (2013) argue that we must be cautious about interpreting an absence of racial group consciousness as an indication of either lack of awareness or denial of the presence of discrimination. While my focus is not on the degree to which racial discourses among Mexicans in Mexico approximate a U.S.-style color-blind ideology, this scholarship informs an understanding of the identities and attitudes immigrants bring from Mexico and how migration may challenge them to adjust their identification.

Mexican Immigrants Negotiating Racial Identities in a U.S. Context

As discussed earlier, scholars frequently interpret the racial identification of Latino immigrants through the historical and contemporary lens of a U.S. racial classification system. For example, researchers often read identification with whiteness as an indication of cultural assimilation into an

American identity, lighter skin color, a reflection of how one is racially classified by others, or all three (Tafoya 2004). However, just as my findings regarding Mexican Americans challenge these assumptions, so too do the narratives of immigrants in the study. For most interviewees who migrated as adults, their understanding of identity was formed primarily in a racial context very different from that in the United States. Nevertheless, immigrant respondents' views of race are at least somewhat informed by their experiences with racial classification and encounters in the United States. My analysis of this process utilizes a constructionist approach (Nagel 1994; Cornell and Hartmann 1997; Jenkins 1997), exploring how these immigrants both respond to external classification and assert their own identities through a process of articulating boundaries, positioning themselves relative to other groups, and learning the new meanings attached to various racial group identities in a U.S. context (Cornell and Hartmann 1997). Most immigrant respondents spoke only Spanish and were shown the Spanish-language version of the U.S. census form; six who interviewed in English answered the standard English version. Throughout the analysis I will not be translating the actual term that respondents use as a self-referent on the form, as these labels may have different meanings in English and Spanish (a topic to receive much more attention in Chapter Five).

Overall, about one-quarter (five) of the twenty-one Mexican immigrant interviewees identified as racially "white" or "*blanca*" on the census, while the majority marked "other race." Nine immigrant respondents identified as "Hispanic" or "Hispano/a," five as "Mexican" or "Mexicano/a," one as "mestizo," and one as "campesino." The last did so as an expression of his identity as an indigenous person who had worked in the fields in a rural community in Mexico. Like Mexican Americans in the study, those who indicate "*blanca*" or "white" for their race are not lighter skinned, and they exhibit similar attachment to their cultural heritage as those who label as "other race."

Some Mexican immigrants also distance themselves from an undesirable racialized identity in the United States by positioning themselves as different from African Americans and lower-income U.S.-born Mexican Americans. But, unlike what I observed among Mexican American respondents, interviews with immigrants do not reveal a straightforward relationship between racial ideology as color-blind or anti-racist and their census racial choices. While I did find evidence of discursive strategies that mirror some aspects of color-blind framing, Mexican immigrants' narratives do not conform to the racial ideology continuum applied to

Mexican Americans in Chapters Two and Three. For example, immigrants who identify formally as "white" do not identify as "American," whereas all "white" Mexican Americans do. Moreover, regardless of racial label preference, Mexican immigrants typically acknowledged racism as a contemporary problem, whether they minimized their personal experiences with discrimination or not. Indeed, asserting a formal racial label on the census is such a fundamentally different process for immigrants compared with U.S.-born Mexican Americans that they warrant a separate analysis.

The first section of this analysis, "From *Raza* to Race," focuses on how immigrants translate their understanding of *raza* in Mexico into U.S. racial categories. While most immigrants identified first and foremost with their nationality as Mexicanos, there are important differences in their class and racial origins in Mexico that also inform their racial choices. The next section, "From Privilege to 'Just Another Mexican,'" explores how two higher-class interviewees adjusted their identities and ideology through the migration process. The third section, "In and Out of Mestizo Identity," explores the identities of the two respondents who identified as "mestizo" and "campesino," detailing their nuanced racial experiences and how migration shapes the way they see themselves in relation to both U.S. racial categories and relative to other Mexican-origin persons in a U.S. context.

From *Raza* to Race

Emilio Contreras, an electrician in his thirties who is from Cuidad Acuña, Mexico, had been living in the United States for less than a year when I interviewed him in his Del Rio home, where he lives with his wife and young daughter. When I showed Emilio the census form, he said: "Well, I have never answered such a form." He explained that he was unsure of what to mark, having never encountered questions like these. After looking over the racial options, Emilio decided to write in "Mexicano" for his race. When I asked him what he thought about other terms such as "Hispanic," he replied: "I don't really know very well the meaning of the word. I don't know if it would fit [me]. A Hispanic, well, I think you call a Hispanic anyone who can speak Spanish." Of the immigrants that I interviewed, Emilio had spent the least amount of time in the United States. His answer provides a glimpse into the initial response that Mexican immigrants may feel when approaching formal racial identification in the United States. Emilio sees his *raza* in terms of his nationality, and he is only beginning to understand the meaning behind panethnic categories such as Hispanic.

In Wendy Roth's (2012) research on Puerto Rican and Dominican immigrants, she finds that her interviewees do not so much adopt new racial identities through migration but rather acquire a new racial schema that coexists alongside their understanding of race from their home country. Similarly, I find that immigrants' understanding of their *raza* as Mexicano/a remains, as they come to understand and assert their "race" in the United States. For example, Silvia Vallegos, a young woman in her twenties who migrated to Del Rio ten years ago, identifies as "Hispano" on the census form. She explains, "Well, I consider myself Mexicana. In this country I say Hispano because I belong to the Spanish-language [group]. But I consider—like, I'm Mexicana, my nationality is Mexicana, and I'm proud to be Mexicana." While more of my immigrant respondents wrote in "Hispanic" or "Hispano/a" for their race on the census, none typically use the term in their daily lives. Rather, they prefer "Mexicano/a." The decision to identify as Hispanic formally, when most immigrants do not otherwise use the term, demonstrates the fluidity of racial identification and the context-specific use of such labels. This finding resonates with research that suggests many immigrants may assert panethnic "Hispanic" identification as "part of a constellation of individuals' multiple identifications," coexisting alongside national-origin labels (Jones-Correa and Leal 1996: 214).

Often in social science research, labels selected on surveys are understood as reflective of a respondent's preferred identity, especially when persons are given the option to write in a response. However, as demonstrated, this is not necessarily the case. Recall Maria's response quoted in the opening to the chapter: that "the form belongs to the U.S. government" and Hispanic describes "people who speak Spanish in the U.S." Silvia and Maria understand that they are part of a Spanish-speaking group that serves as their "racial" identity in a U.S. context. Thus, they respond with U.S. racial terminology, even though they feel little connection to the term.

Silvia actually spoke at length of her pride in her Mexican heritage and preference for her children to identify themselves as Mexican despite growing up in the United States. She says:

Well, I want them to become conscious that they are from a Mexican family. That we are Mexican. Just because we live here, I don't want to say—I think that this country has positive aspects but also many negative aspects. Us Mexicans, we're—we have different customs. We are like a family, very united. Like, everything that is positive in the people of Mexico, that is what I want them to take with them. Our roots, to not forget their culture, all of it. But in this country, I think that it is a country of opportunity. I hope they see their opportunities, while also try to help the people, to never see themselves as above people. I hope that if you [*here she speaks as if talking to her children*] that you help them, to not look down on them. To try to get ahead, and try to give to this country. To be a good example, to not say, "Hey! These Mexicans, they only come and do this and this and this." No, we should shed that part—we should be the aspects [of our culture that are] most positive.

Silvia's comments regarding her desires for her children highlight several important themes. In addition to wishing that her children identify with their Mexican roots, she expresses an underlying fear that I found among many immigrants: that their children would look down on Mexican immigrants, positioning themselves above them. Her comments further reflect her belief that Mexican immigrants and Mexican Americans should align themselves in support of each other. When immigrant respondents used the terms "Hispanic" or "Hispano/a" in discussing their experiences, it was often a way to group themselves with U.S.-born Mexican Americans, a topic I discuss in greater detail in Chapter Five. Here, Silvia's identification as "Hispano" on the form can further be interpreted as an expression of this desire.

Yet, while professing a strong pride in her Mexican heritage and a wish for collaboration, Silvia believes that Mexicans often hold each other back. She is critical of what she believes is a tendency toward jealousy among Mexicans. When I asked about her experiences with discrimination, she responded:

If we see a Mexican trying to better himself, or studying, or wanting to get ahead, these same Mexicans [*smacks her hand down with the other*]. And it's not, it's not to say—sometimes we get more support from an American than from our own race. But, I think that it shouldn't be like that. If a Mexican wants to get ahead, they should work hard to. So that they don't say that Mexicans—like, how can we make our race greater doing positive things? But I have seen more discrimination within our own race.

Whereas Mexican Americans who identify as "other race" in the study spoke of personal experiences with prejudice and mistreatment from

Anglos, Silvia was dismissive of discrimination from outsiders. Instead, she emphasizes that she sees more discrimination among persons of Mexican origin.

While most immigrants acknowledge racism as a contemporary problem, persons like Silvia, Maria, and Emilio, who had been in the United States for ten years or less and spoke little to no English, were often less likely to say that they had personally experienced discrimination from other racial groups. A few reasons may account for this. First, immigrants with greater English fluency and more time in the United States may have had more opportunity to interact with other racial groups, leading to a greater possibility of encountering racist comments or attitudes from others. Second, recent arrivals anticipate that they will be treated as outsiders and hence may have differing expectations with regard to how others respond to them. For example, Viruell-Fuentes (2007) found that first-generation Mexican immigrant women reported fewer incidents of discriminatory encounters than their U.S.-born counterparts. She cites segregation, a language barrier, and differences in expectations for treatment as explanation for this disparity.

Overall, most immigrant interviewees understood their racial place in the United States to be under this "Hispanic" label. In the absence of a "Hispanic" racial category, however, a few attempted to locate themselves vis-à-vis the existing options provided. Only one immigrant respondent (Alma), who will be discussed in the next section, was adamant about her whiteness. Four others who selected *"blanca"* for their race were much more tentative in their response, stating that they usually identified as Hispanic on forms and Mexicano/a in their daily lives. Indeed, none of those who identified as *"blanca"* ever used the term, or other Spanish words such as *"güero/a,"* to describe themselves or their skin color outside the context of the census form. Moreover, no immigrant interviewees who selected *"blanca"* were phenotypically white. This finding regarding skin color resembles that in my interviews with Mexican Americans. However, whereas Mexican Americans claim whiteness to assert their American identities and defend themselves against discrimination, this was not the case for most immigrants. The process of selecting *"blanca"* for immigrants was more akin to a student taking a multiple-choice exam who does not know the correct answer and attempts to determine the best choice through a process of elimination. These respondents did not immediately choose *"blanca."* Rather, they continued, ruling out other possibilities before hesitantly indicating their choice.

Ines Flores provides a perfect example of this. Ines is in her early fifties and had been living in the United States for twenty-two years at the time that we spoke. She lives in Del Rio, where she works serving food in a cafeteria. Ines responded to the race question by stating that she is "Hispana," but upon seeing no such racial category, she opted to mark *"blanca,"* explaining: "Because *negra*—I don't go [there], [*pauses and looks over other racial options listed, shaking her head at each one*] so I am *blanca* . . . but usually [I answer] Hispana, nothing more." Ines chooses whiteness as the best fit because she does not see herself reflected in any of the other options. However, it is important to note that it is a denial of blackness specifically that she verbalizes when she articulates her choice. While Ines did not express any negativity towards African Americans or blackness, her response does signify a distancing maneuver. Immigrants may position themselves closer to whiteness in their attempts to resist the stigma of racialization in the United States (Murguía and Foreman 2003) and also as an extension of the racial hierarchies of their home countries (Jones-Correa 1998). The elevation of whiteness and devaluation of darker skin or blackness are a part of Mexico's racial discourse (Sue 2013). Thus, these immigrants' identification with whiteness can also be seen as a reflection of the dominant racial narrative of Mexico that elevates whiteness over indigenous roots and typically elides the presence of blackness entirely.

As previously noted, despite this emphasis on a shared *raza* as national origin in Mexico, some Mexican immigrants do come from relative racial and class privilege. Many immigrants I interviewed were working low-wage jobs and had come from lower-income backgrounds in Mexico. But I also interviewed a few who were from elite and middle-class backgrounds and an indigenous migrant. The next two sections explore how variation in the racial and class subjectivities of interviewees in Mexico shapes how they assert racial identities in a U.S. context.

From Privilege to "Just Another Mexican"

Alma Fuentes is from an affluent family in Mexico City. She migrated to the United States in the mid-1960s to attend college in California. There, she met and married a Mexican American man whom she followed to Del Rio, Texas, nearly three decades ago. Alma is now divorced, in her early fifties, and the mother of two grown children. She became a U.S. citizen years ago but states that she will always consider herself a Mexicana. Alma indicated her Mexican ancestry under the Hispanic-origin question on the census and says "Hispanic" is also a term that she uses to label herself here in the United States. For her race, however, Alma stated unequivocally that she is white. Unlike U.S.-born Mexican Americans in Chapter Two who claim whiteness on the census to assert their American identities, Alma does not see herself as American. Her white identity long preceded her migration to the United States. She explains: "Because in Mexico I was always white. And when I came across [to] the United States, I didn't become brown or anything else." Yet, Alma's skin is in fact brown. It is not color but class that marked Alma as white, or *güera*, in Mexico. Her inclination to create a boundary distinguishing herself from less economically privileged Mexicans is rooted primarily in her experiences growing up in Mexico City. She remembers vividly how when she was a young girl, her mother became angry with her because she danced with a boy who was below the family's social stature. He was of *"la gente del pueblo"* her mother had told her. While the phrase literally translates as "people from town," Alma remembers it as an expression used to describe both lower-class and indigenous Mexicans.

Alma feels that her family's elite social standing in Mexico separates her from many Mexican immigrants and Mexican Americans in the United States. She notes, however, that people typically fail to recognize this difference, viewing her as "just another Mexican." Her children also face such racialization. Moreover, Alma laments that despite their being born and raised in the United States, her children are seen as Mexican American, rather than as simply American. She says, "I think Mexican American should actually be American of Mexican descent because we do not see Italian American, German American, and so. . . . It should be American of Mexican descent—American." Alma attempts to counter the discrimination her children face by instilling in them a sense of pride in their heritage and by emphasizing with them that they are not like lower-class Mexican Americans. She says:

> [I tell my children] the family that we came from, my family was—my background goes back to about five generations ago. This lady was a sister to one of the viceroys in Mexico, and that's from my father's tree. They, my mother's tree—I have people very much involved in Mexican government. And I want them to know not only that money is important, but your values, education, and where they come from on my side.

Alma wants her children to achieve a higher status in the United States, something comparable to the status of her family in Mexico. However, she believes Mexican Americans in the United States have leveled aspirations, with little desire for such economic advancement. She feels that her son has taken on these characteristics, while her daughter is more ambitious. Alma explains, "My son who is more Mexican American has a degree and everything, but he would rather just teach. He could get a job for forty to fifty thousand dollars, but no. My daughter who is more anglicized, she will go for a better job." On the surface, it may appear that Alma's remarks reflect a desire for her children to assimilate culturally, to become more Anglo-American. Yet, Alma stresses her desire that they maintain their Spanish-speaking skills and identification with their Mexican heritage. She explains that it is not Mexican culture and values that she wishes for them to disavow but what she sees as Mexican American attitudes. Throughout the interview, Alma made remarks distancing herself and her children from both lower-income Mexican Americans and Mexican immigrants, as well as from African Americans. She frequently blamed these groups for their lower status, saying that they did not wish to advance economically. She wants to distance herself and her children from these characteristics, and so she aligns herself with whiteness. Thus, even though others do not accept her or her children as racially white in the United States, Alma asserts a white identity on the census.

Alma's comments reveal many similarities with Mexican Americans in the extreme "Race is no barrier" position on the racial ideology continuum (Chapter Two) who espouse a meritocratic philosophy and distance themselves from lower-class persons and those who claim racial difference from the dominant majority. However, there are also important differences in identification and ideology that separate Alma from self-identified "white" U.S.-born Mexican Americans. First, even though she wishes her children were seen as simply American, she does not identify herself as "American." In contrast, all "white" Mexican Americans strongly assert their American identities. Second, "white" Mexican Americans invariably place all Mexican Americans in the white racial category, including those who are lower income and dark skinned. Alma sees herself as white but definitely does not see all or even most Mexican immigrants or Mexican Americans as in that category. Finally, "white" Mexican Americans did not typically feel they were ever seen by others as white, and they identified as such only on census forms and not in their daily lives. Whereas for Mexican Americans, whiteness is a defensive posture used in public racial identification, Alma was white in Mexico for the first twenty years of her life. Thus, her whiteness is both an extension of her class-privileged background in Mexico and a way of constructing a boundary between herself and a stigmatizing racialized identity in the United States.

Pablo Ceballos also comes from a privileged family in Mexico City, but unlike Alma, migrating to the United States resulted in a change in both his racial ideology and identification. In Mexico, Pablo explains that he considered himself and his family to be white. Pablo has a tan/olive skin tone, but he notes that his mother and brothers are very fair and that none of his relatives are dark skinned. A combination of both color and class mark his family as "*güeros*" in Mexico City. He says:

> Some people that are Mexican look like really brown. Sometimes people think if I look like this color or brown or something, they say I'm Mexican, Latino, Hispanic. It's a little confusing because all my brothers in my family are like white, with green eyes, blue eyes—my granddad is green eyed and my mom is blue eyed.

A graduate of the Universidad Nacional Autónoma de México (UNAM), Pablo is in his midthirties and operates a Mexican restaurant in the Dallas area. He speaks English, though not fluently, and is a legal resident. At the time we spoke, he had been living in the United States for sixteen years. Pablo says that coming from an economically advantaged background in Mexico, he never really thought a lot about social inequality. While he acknowledges that prejudice exists in Mexico along both class and color lines, he never felt the sting of discrimination himself there. Like Alma, here in the United States he has experienced a shift in how he is seen by others. While he is not dark skinned, his olive skin tone, facial features, and most importantly his thick accent mark him as "Hispanic" in the United States. Noticing how he and other immigrants are treated, particularly more recent arrivals and those who do not speak English, has made Pablo think more critically about inequality. He has been especially bothered by how U.S.-born Mexican Americans sometimes distance themselves from new immigrants. Describing his hopes for his two young children here in the United States, he says:

> Well, I would like that they learn to be hardworking people, responsible, and, well, that they help the people who come [to the United States] because many kids born here don't want to help when they see those who have the same face that come from Mexico. Those who come oftentimes don't receive much help. So, to help, be responsible, to make them feel welcome, and to know that they are Mexican too. To help and not to be ashamed [that they are Mexican].

Unlike Alma, who responds to racialization in the United States by asserting whiteness and creating a boundary between herself and lower-class immigrants and Mexican Americans, Pablo reacts in the opposite manner. He identifies with lower-class immigrants with whom he shares this experience of being stereotyped in the United States. Pablo wrote in "Hispanic" for his race on the census, although the term is not something he uses to describe himself outside the context of formal identification; rather, he typically uses Mexicano. But like Maria and Silvia, mentioned in previous sections, Pablo understands that formal identification in the United States is intended to reflect U.S. racial categories. It has been made clear to him since his arrival that whiteness in the United States is tied to both white skin color and U.S. citizenship. Speaking of his lighter skin tone, he notes, "Because some people just think this color is like American people . . . but nobody ever thinks, 'Oh, it's Mexican.'" Pablo has come to understand that color and class descriptors like "*güero*" and "*blanco*" in Mexico are not the same as the racial category "white" in the United States. In translating his identity, he adjusts not only the terms he uses to describe himself but his outlook on racial inequality more generally.

The examples of Alma and Pablo illustrate how Mexican immigrants from more privileged economic backgrounds in Mexico find their "whiteness" challenged by a different meaning given to white identity in the United States. Similar to U.S.-born Mexican American respondents, how they respond to experiences with racialization in the United States is key to how they assert racial identities. Alma reacts defensively, constructing barriers between herself and lower-income immigrants and Mexican Americans, while Pablo makes connections aligning with these groups. Their stories reveal how a privileged position in Mexico leads to a very different orientation to racial classification in the United States than that of lower-class immigrants. The next section further highlights variation among Mexican immigrants, comparing the accounts of two respondents who identified differently in relation to the construction of mestizo identity in Mexico.

In and Out of Mestizo Identity

Marisol Ruiz, a Del Rio resident in her early fifties, is from a large urban area in Central Mexico. She completed high school and considered college, before marrying her husband and starting a family. Her husband is college educated and was professionally employed in Mexico. They left Mexico in the 1980s following the devaluation of the peso, looking for better work opportunities in the United States. In asserting her race on the census, Marisol articulates the dominant racial narrative in Mexico, stating that Mexicans are all mestizos. My conversation with Marisol about her decision to write in "mestiza" for her race went as follows:

> Marisol: I am mestiza, because all in Mexico are mestizos. We are Spanish with Indian [ancestry]. In my distant past . . . because my grandfather is Spanish Spanish and my grandmother. But, in any case we are mestizos in Mexico. All.
>
> JAD: All people or all from your family?
>
> Marisol: All, no. Almost all, except those recently arrived who came from other countries.

The term "mestizo" indicates a person with a mixture of Spanish and indigenous ancestry. As alluded to in Chapter One, in the context of the United States, the term has been used by Mexican American activists as a way of embracing their indigenous roots and rejecting a politics of assimilation, of courting whiteness (Anzaldúa 1987; Marquez 2003; Gutiérrez 2009). For example, Luisa in Chapter Three overcame the shame she had associated with being Mexican American and came to identify as racially Hispanic, articulating her multiracial roots in Mexico as not only Spanish but indigenous. But while in the United States, "mestizo" became a term associated with civil rights and accepting indigeneity, in Mexico the term has a different connotation. "Mestizo" in Mexico is not a radical term for embracing one's indigeneity; it is a term used by the majority that separates them from Indians in Mexico. Notice in Marisol's remarks that while she is asserting a mestiza identity, she emphasizes her Spanish roots, describing her grandparents as "Spanish Spanish." The rhetoric of *mestizaje* is one of acknowledgement of indigeneity but ultimately a whitening tale, where the result is understood to be more Spanish. Hence, with her identification as mestiza, and emphasis on her Spanish heritage, Marisol is actually in fact distancing herself from Indian Mexicans. Indeed, there is no acknowledgement in her comments regarding the racial composition of Mexico that allow for the indigenous (or Afro-origin) populations. Rather, by her account all Mexicans are mestizos.

While Marisol's remarks minimize racial difference in Mexico, she articulates an understanding of the history of racial barriers in the United States. She associates the term "Chicano" with the civil rights movement for Mexicans, explaining:

They tried to better treatment of Mexicans because they [Mexicans] were treated worse than the blacks, even though no one talks about it. Many of the blacks complain a lot about how they suffered bitterly, but Mexicans were also oppressed.

Here, Marisol articulates the painful racialized history that Mexican people in the United States have faced. However, also implicit in her remarks is a critique of African Americans, who Marisol believes are not interested in making progress but rather dwelling on their history of oppression. Because of these perceptions, Marisol wishes to distance herself from African Americans. For example, when asked about her dating preferences for her children, Marisol says:

For me, I don't want them to marry persons who are the color black because . . . It's not that I'm discriminating, [but that] they are not going to be able to rise above the cultural differences. Then they'll have a lot of problems. . . . There are differences [between the groups] in culture, habits, and ways of thinking. And in the end, I don't think it would be a good relationship. I want them [my children] to marry someone good and decent.

When I probed Marisol further, she explained that she would prefer that her children not date Mexicans in the United States either because "they have changed a lot." She does not like the attitudes of Mexican Americans and African Americans, preferring that her children marry someone Anglo or Asian. In her narrative, she cites "cultural" differences as the reason why she would prefer her children not date African Americans, and yet, Asians and Anglos also represent other "cultures"—ones that are more palatable to Marisol. Her comments here very much resonate with a color-blind ideological frame of "cultural racism" discussed in Chapter Two, where persons use alternate terminology, avoiding sounding racist by focusing on "culture" in lieu of naming race (Bonilla-Silva 2010).

In the end, however, her reference to wanting her children to marry "good and decent" people reveals her belief that African Americans do not meet these criteria. Her identification and accompanying ideological framework are those of a privileged position as a middle-class woman who sees herself reflected in the dominant racial narrative of Mexico. For her, identifying as mestiza can be seen as a way to hold onto that identification, resisting grouping herself with Mexican Americans as racially

"Hispanic" on the census form. This use of mestizo identity directly contrasts the use of the term among Mexican American activists as a celebration of racial mixture and the reclamation of indigeneity.

Estevan Parra was on the other end of the class and race spectrum in Mexico, living in a rural indigenous community in Michoacán. He immigrated to the United States in the early 1980s to look for work. In Mexico, he went to school only through the third grade, which he said was very common in the area where he lived. He lives in Fort Worth, where he has worked in various factory jobs assembling car parts, radios, and other equipment. Estevan speaks very little English and is not a U.S. citizen, but he does hope to become one someday. When asked what he would answer for his race, Estevan said, "Like there [in my home in Mexico], the race we are . . . we would say, 'We are campesinos.' . . . There are many Indians in my land. There, we call ourselves campesinos." The term "campesino" literally means a person from "*el campo*" (the country) and is used to mean someone who farms or works in the fields. However, the term is also associated with indigenous communities in some parts of Mexico (Lerner 1979). Estevan has a dark red-brown complexion and facial features that are typically associated with Indian ancestry. He says that in the area where he lived in Mexico, they were mostly Indians, and they began working in the fields from a young age. He was even involved in some protests involving worker's rights in his hometown before his migration to the United States. Estevan's identification as "campesino" is an affirmation of his identity as an Indian and his experience as a field-worker.

In the United States, Estevan's social world now consists of other Mexican immigrants who also work factory jobs. He still sees himself as different—identifying with his indigenous heritage and history in Mexico, but he also now shares many similar experiences with mestizo migrants. He and his friends encounter discrimination from employers and in other settings. Estevan specifically recalls how he was fired from his job by a boss who he says was prejudiced against Mexicans. He recalls, "I had this job nine years ago and they changed bosses—an Italian man became the boss and I lost my job. And then the Italian left, and my boss returned. I got my job back."

Estevan's experiences with adjustment to racialization in the United States are quite different from those of Alma, Pablo, and Marisol. In Mexico, Estevan occupied a marginalized position relative to mestizo Mexicans. In the United States, however, he is now grouped with them, as most Americans see him as simply Mexican. The marked contrast between his experience and that of Marisol demonstrates how one's orientation toward the mestizo majority in Mexico has an impact on the experience of racial classification and ideology in the migration process.

Conclusion

Much sociological literature has focused on how racial identities are transformed and altered through the process of migration as immigrants struggle to place themselves racially in a new country with potentially different racial markers and categories (Oboler 1995; Rodríguez 2000; Newby and Dowling 2007; Roth 2010, 2012). While some have interpreted Latino formal identification with whiteness or racial "otherness" as reflective of assimilation and integration similar to the meaning of such identities in a U.S. racial paradigm (Yancey 2003; Tafoya 2004), a number of scholars have suggested that Latinos view racial identification in ways that differ substantially from U.S. standards (Rodríguez 2000; Roth 2010, 2012). My findings with regard to Mexican immigrants' racial identification on the census concur with many of the themes presented by Roth (2010, 2012) and Rodríguez (2000), particularly that Latino immigrants' formal identification is often not a direct reflection of skin color. Moreover, similar to these studies that primarily focus on Caribbeans and South Americans, I find Mexican immigrants understand their racial identities as fundamentally tied to both national origin and experiences with racial assignment in the United States. The overwhelming majority of Mexican immigrants in the study see themselves as Mexicanos/as first and foremost. Indeed, identifications as racially "Hispanic" or "white" on the census do not typically reflect the actual terms most immigrants use to describe themselves in daily life. Rather, these racial choices represent attempts to provide the "correct" answer on the form by conforming to how they feel they are expected to answer such questions.

Not all immigrants approach racial classification in the United States from the same vantage point, as differences in their class and racial identities in Mexico further shape this process. For more middle-class and elite migrants, coming to the United States means losing aspects of their privileged positions, as in the United States they are grouped with lower-class Mexican immigrants and Mexican Americans as "just another Mexican." This process can either strengthen their resolve to distance themselves from a stigmatizing racial identity (Alma and Marisol) or lead them to amend their ideology and identification toward aligning themselves with such racialized communities (Pablo). Like Mexican Americans, racial ideology and positioning relative to other groups can inform racial choices for some immigrants, particularly those with lengthier histories in the United States. My respondents' stories reveal both the critical role of specific racial and class origins in Mexico in constructing identity in the United States and the disconnect between formal and everyday labeling among Mexican immigrants. Chapter Five will now further explore racial identification outside the realm of formal classification for both Mexican immigrants and Mexican Americans, as they assert their identities in daily life contextually through the use of multiple identity labels.

"That's what we call ourselves here": Mexican Americans and Mexican Immigrants Negotiating Racial Labeling in Daily Life

Mike Vargas, an accountant in Fort Worth, Texas, identifies in a variety of ways in his daily life, each of which is subtly dependent on audience, language, and context. His mother is a second-generation Mexican American, while his father's family dates back at least four generations in Texas. Mike usually identifies as "Hispanic," a term that he defines as someone of Mexican ancestry who was born in the United States. At times, he also calls himself "Mexican American," but he explains that he is not "Mexican" because he is not an immigrant. When someone insults people of Mexican heritage in his presence, however, he asserts a "Mexican" identity strategically in that context. Moreover, when he is speaking Spanish, he refers to himself as "Mexicano." But Mike is also definitely an "American," and he never uses "Latino" because "it sounds like someone who isn't from here." He is a "Texan," but he would not typically use the Spanish corollary "Tejano" as a self-referent because he associates the term with styles of music and working-class cultural expressions among Mexican Americans in Texas that do not suit him. Yet, when someone asks in Spanish where he is from, "*Soy* Tejano [I am Tejano]" is his response. So, in sum, Mike is Mexicano but not Mexican, Texan but not really Tejano, and Hispanic because he is not an immigrant. To outsiders this might seem confusing and even rather contradictory. However, among Mexican Americans in the study I found remarkable consistency in many of the distinctions in labeling that Mike identifies here. In this chapter I move beyond formal classification to explore the multiple labels that my respondents use in their day-to-day lives and how these identity assertions vary depending upon context and audience.

The Multiple Meanings of Latino/Hispanic Identities

The federal government defines the categories "Hispanic" and "Latino" similarly as inclusive of all persons of Spanish-speaking origin (Ennis et al. 2011). However, the various uses of these panethnic labels are far more complicated, as both have racial and political connotations as well. Indeed, the labels "Hispanic" and "Latino" are frequently used throughout the United States to describe persons who are "brown" (Alcoff 2000; Rodríguez 2000; Itzigsohn 2004). As Clara Rodríguez (2000) notes, the fact that Latino persons who appear phenotypically white are often referred to as "light skinned" and not as white demonstrates the ways in which Latinos are continually racialized.

This shared experience of racialization among many Latinos can lead to the use of panethnicity to unite Latino national-origin groups in addressing discrimination. Latino/Hispanic identity may emerge situationally for such political purposes, particularly in locations with diverse Latino populations (Padilla 1985; De Genova and Ramos-Zayas 2003). For example, in a study of Latino panethnicity in Chicago, Felix Padilla (1985) found that Latino identification was evoked as a goal-specific organizing tool that linked Mexicans and Puerto Ricans together in their common struggle against racial discrimination in housing. Padilla noted that this Latino panethnic identity was based less on perceptions of cultural similarity than on a shared positionality relative to the dominant society. Moreover, this panethnic identity did not replace national-origin identification as Mexican or Puerto Rican.

De Genova and Ramos-Zayas' (2003) Chicago-based research further supports the finding that Latinos identify primarily in terms of their national origin and that assertions of Latino identity result from structural forces. They found that when the "Latino" label emerged, it was constructed as a "racial formation" that evolved from the discrimination faced by Latinos. De Genova and Ramos-Zayas (2003: 177) write: ". . . the durable meaningfulness of that Latino commonality of identity or interest was derived, first and foremost, from its location within a racialized social order in the U.S. that was defined by the placement of Latinos in relation to whites and Blacks." Thus, both studies highlight how Latino identification develops from racialization in the United States, and in specific contexts may further reflect political moves to unite Latinos in the face of discrimination.[1]

Yet, while the terms "Hispanic" and "Latino" may more generally refer to a Spanish-speaking "brown" racialized category in the United States, the meanings and uses of these labels vary significantly by region. In some locales, specifically in the Southwest, the term "Hispanic" is used colloquially to designate persons of Mexican ancestry who were born in the United States. In New Mexico, for example, the category of Hispanic or Hispano is often used to refer to residents who are Spanish speaking but whose ancestors date back many generations in the state (Nieto-Philips 2004). Similarly in Texas, Hispanic identity is tied to Mexican origin (Mindiola et al. 2002) and is often used to describe U.S.-born Mexican Americans specifically (Dowling 2005). The relatively low percentage of other Latino groups in both Texas and New Mexico contributes to such an exclusive definition of Hispanic identity as Mexican-origin only. This creates problems for the small number of Afro-Cuban and other non-Mexican Latinos in both states who may find themselves excluded from the category "Hispanic" (Newby and Dowling 2007; Dowling and Newby 2010). Thus, in addition to serving as a unifying identity, the Hispanic label may also be used as a boundary marker separating Mexican-origin persons from other Latinos and even differentiating Mexican Americans from Mexican immigrants in some regions.[2]

Mexican Americans and Mexican Immigrants: Labels That Divide and Unite

Research on labeling distinctions within the Mexican-origin population further reveals that Mexican Americans and Mexican immigrants differ substantially in the types of identity labels they assert (Hurtado et al. 1994; Gutiérrez 1995; Richardson 1999; Vila 2000). Mexican immigrants have been found to be more likely to accept labels like "Mexican" and "foreigner," while second- and third-generation Mexican Americans are more likely to identify as "American" (Hurtado et al. 1994). Additionally, both groups further construct their identities in dialogue with, and often in opposition to, each other (Vila 2000). Mexican Americans frequently complain that Anglos lump all persons of Mexican ancestry together, conflating Mexican origin with a lower-class immigrant identity (Macias 2006; Jiménez 2010). To combat this, some U.S.-born Mexican Americans attempt to distinguish themselves from working-class, recent immigrants through the use of distancing maneuvers. For example, in Vila's (2000) study of Mexican Americans and Mexican immigrants in El Paso, Texas, he notes specifically how both of these groups utilize discursive strategies he terms "narrative plots" or storylines that embody ideological frameworks for constructing identities. In particular, he finds that Mexican Americans frequently assign negative attributes to Mexico and Mexican immigrants, employing an "all poverty is Mexican" narrative plot that serves to construct a boundary between their identities as Mexican Americans and an undesirable association with Mexico (Vila 2000, 2003).

Vila's research particularly reveals how the U.S.-Mexico border is a site where enhanced border security and enforcement further translates into the fortification of social boundaries between Mexican Americans and Mexican immigrants. Vila (2003: 138) notes: "For Mexican Americans living on the U.S. side of the border, the *source* of their difference is always present, a constant reminder. This is not true for Mexicans living elsewhere in the country. Thus Mexicans living on the border are dealing with the meaning of their identity as an ethnicity and as a nationality simultaneously." Mexican Americans across the country face a perpetual assumption from others that they are foreigners and not Americans (Macias 2006; Jiménez 2010). At the same time, they encounter scrutiny within the Mexican-origin community, as more acculturated Mexican Americans confront questions of authenticity and belonging (Vila 2000; Ochoa 2004; García Bedolla 2005; Vasquez 2011). On the border, however, both these issues are magnified (Vila 2000, 2003). Among my respondents, I find many resolve this tension by presenting themselves differently in various situations, dependent upon context and audience.

The fluid dynamics of labeling among Mexican Americans and Mexican immigrants are deeply embedded in a larger social structure of the dominant white racial frame, where racialized minorities are systematically devalued (Feagin 2010). The stigma placed on nonwhite immigrants and U.S. racial minorities strongly influences the identification of both Mexican Americans and Mexican immigrants. Mexican Americans in the study reject the label "Mexican" in large part because they wish to distance themselves from the negative attributes associated with immigrants who are stereotyped as low income and "illegal." Moreover, as the previous chapter explored, Mexican immigrants can similarly disassociate themselves from U.S.-born Mexican Americans, as they come to see racialized minorities in the United States as occupying a disadvantaged position. Labels can either express this separation between these groups or reveal moments of political alignment. For example, Mike, introduced at the beginning of this chapter, is adamant that he is "American" and not "Mexican," and he particularly emphasizes his "American" identity in situations where he feels he is racially profiled. However, in a context where he hears a racist remark against Mexican immigrants, he adopts the label "Mexican" in solidarity with them.

Fluidity in ethnic label-choice is often associated with what has been termed "situational ethnicity." Waters' (1990) interviews with multigenerational European Americans reveal how ethnic identity is largely situational for her respondents and not a salient part of their lives. Most have not experienced any discrimination because of their identities as Irish, Italian, or German. These identities are voluntary, surface only intermittently, and have no social costs or impact on their day-to-day lives. Thus, fluidity in ethnic labeling for European Americans has been found to be reflective of the flexible and costless nature of their ethnic identities (Waters 1990).

In stark contrast, Mexican Americans and Mexican immigrants in the study do not enjoy a flexible and costless ethnic identity. Rather, for my respondents, fluidity in labeling coexists alongside racial constraints. My findings in this regard resonate with Gilda Ochoa's (2004) study of Mexican Americans in La Puente, California. Contrasting the experiences of her interviewees to those of Waters (1990), Ochoa (2004: 97) writes: "Institutions, ideologies, and individuals may structure, limit, and constrain Mexican Americans' life chances such that their identities often are not optional, not voluntary, and not temporary." Similarly, I find that my Mexican American respondents' racial identities are highly salient in their lives, as most relay stories of racial discrimination. Mexican Americans in the study develop strategies to deal with these experiences by positioning themselves either alongside or in opposition to immigrants.

Ochoa (2004) characterizes Mexican Americans' attitudes toward Mexican immigrants as reflecting a "conflict-solidarity continuum." On one end of this ideological continuum are those Mexican Americans who adopt a power-conflict perspective, aligning themselves with immigrants and supporting policies such as language accommodations. On the other side are those Mexican Americans who espouse assimilationist views, believing immigrants should adapt to the language and customs of the dominant culture. Ochoa finds that those who adopt the power-conflict perspective are more likely to embrace the label "Chicano" with its connection to political activism. Indeed, for these individuals, this identity often specifically evolved through a process of becoming politicized about challenging racial oppression. However, those who identify as "Chicano" are among a minority of her respondents, while the majority identify as Mexican American, alone or in combination with other labels such as Hispanic or Latino. Ochoa does not find that her respondents' labeling preferences as Mexican American vs. Hispanic or Latino directly correspond to differences in their politics. Rather, she notes that respondents in both ideological camps often use a range of labels in daily life (Ochoa 2004).

Similar to Ochoa, I do not find that identifying with the terms "Mexican American" vs. "Hispanic" as primary or secondary identifiers corresponds to differences in the racial politics of my interviewees. Rather, respondents across the ideological spectrum often utilize multiple terms. However, what I do find is that *how* and *when* both Mexican American and immigrant respondents use these labels in their narratives reflect the deployment of specific discursive strategies that are linked to racial ideology.

The first section of the analysis, "The Meaning of 'Mexican' for Mexican Americans," explores how many Mexican Americans define and position themselves relative to this label. The next section, "'Only when I'm speaking Spanish': Identity Labels That Shift in Translation," then focuses on how Mexican Americans change the labels they use dependent upon to whom they are speaking and in what language. Here, I discuss how language alters the significance of words, such that Mexicano and Tejano embody very different meanings in their uses than their literal translations: Mexican and Texan. The final section, "Contrasting Uses of 'Panethnic' Labels for Mexican Americans and Mexican Immigrants," explores how Mexican immigrants and Mexican Americans differ substantially in the meanings they assign to various terms, particularly the labels "Hispanic" and "Latino." By exposing these divergent and contextual uses of these labels, my interviews reveal a complex portrait of racial labeling in daily life and how racial ideology informs this process.

The Meaning of "Mexican" for Mexican Americans

I vividly remember a conversation I had with a Mexican American student during my time working as an instructor at the University of Texas at Austin. After explaining that I was researching how persons of Mexican origin identify themselves, he responded quite strongly, stating: "I don't like anyone calling me Mexican. I see it as a slur; it's like calling a black person the 'n' word. They wouldn't call a black person that, would they? No, they would say black or African American. It's the same thing. I don't want to be called Mexican; I want to be called Hispanic or Mexican American." While the analogy is extreme, this very powerful anecdote best conveys just how offended many Mexican Americans feel when others, especially Anglos, call them "Mexican." Mexican Americans in the study relayed numerous stories of encounters where they were assumed to be immigrants. Many were bothered by these experiences, viewing such incidents as an affront to their American identities and family history in the United States. Moreover, because Mexican immigrants are stereotyped as lower income and undocumented, these moments of mistaken identity often translate into assumptions that they do not speak English or cannot afford expensive items at stores. Hence, for Mexican Americans, "Mexican" is an undesirable label precisely because of the stigma it carries.

Respondents across the racial ideology continuum rejected the label "Mexican," including both self-identified "white" interviewees and those who marked "other race." Respondents on the "white" side of the continuum were often more vocal about their opposition to the term. One such individual is Del Rio resident Irene Hernandez, introduced in Chapter Two, who is in the extreme "Race is no barrier" position on the continuum. Irene firmly believes that calling attention to racial difference hinders Mexican Americans' progress. Instead, she advocates claiming whiteness as the best way to be seen as fully American. Given Irene's ideological stance, it is no surprise that she adamantly opposes the use of "Mexican" as a self-referent both for herself and other Mexican Americans. Irene says:

People say, "Are you Mexican?" I say, "No, because I wasn't born in Mexico." I was born in the United States. My mom and dad were born in the United States. My grandma and grandpa were born in the United States. My culture I would venture to say is . . . Mexican and that's my culture, the culture that I claim. But I am not a Mexican. If I was to go to Mexico and tell them that I am a Mexican, they don't let me buy property over there because I am not Mexican. They don't let me vote because I am not Mexican. Therefore, in my opinion, only ignorant [Mexican American] people [call themselves "Mexican"]. . . . People that know the history of Mexico know that if you cannot vote in that country, then you are not a citizen of that country, then why do you call yourself Mexican?

While she is proud of her Mexican culture, being called a "Mexican" is offensive to Irene as it denies her extensive family history as a sixth-generation Mexican American. Her allusion to not being perceived as Mexican by Mexican citizens adds another dimension to her rejection of the term. Mexican Americans often face scrutiny from Mexican immigrants regarding their authenticity as "Mexican" (Vila 2000; Ochoa 2004; García Bedolla 2005). As discussed earlier, close proximity to the border can heighten this division (Vila 2000). Living in a border town, the meaning of "Mexican" for Irene is very much tied to Mexican citizenship, something that she clearly does not possess. She prefers to identify as Mexican American but adds, "And I would reverse it. I would say I am an American with Mexican descent." Placing "American" first emphasizes her nationality and desire that she and her family be recognized as legitimate citizens of this country.

Mari Bedahl, also in the "Race is no barrier" position on the continuum, is a teacher in the Dallas area. Like Irene, she prefers to be called Mexican American. Mari says:

> Well, I was not born in Mexico, and I am very much an American. I love my country. I would not settle in Mexico. I love to visit it, but I am very proud of my country, so therefore I am Mexican American. You really have to label people what they are. And that's how I understand how Chinese Americans might feel, that live here and have always lived here and love their country. And I know exactly how they feel. I love my country. And I don't like it when in our group [referring to a primarily Latino social club she belongs to] . . . I can't stand for them to start criticizing the United States. And we have some Germans in that group, and they are the ones that are very critical of the United States. And one time they had this heated discussion about the American government and I got up and said, well, the Mexican government was worse. And they realized that they were putting down a country that I love very much and they have to remember that this is my country. And those are things that can set me on fire because I am very loyal to my country. That is why when you ask if I'm Mexican, I say, "No, I'm not Mexican from Mexico," because I've always been here. I was born here.

As a third-generation Mexican American, it is understandable that Mari would see herself as an "American" and not "Mexican." But, as illustrated in Chapter Two, her assertions of Americanness and whiteness also serve as defensive strategies. Mari discussed multiple episodes of discrimination: her college roommate refused to share a room with her, people frequently assume she is lower class, and she feels that she faces harsher scrutiny from her coworkers and parents at the school where she works. Both she and Irene attempt to ward off discrimination by minimizing racial differences and aligning with the dominant white majority. Distancing themselves from Mexican immigrants and "Mexican" identification can further be seen as a part of this process.

Mari refers to herself throughout the interview as "Mexican American" or "Hispanic." In the moments where she details her experiences with discrimination, however, she becomes "Mexican" in the narrative. This occurs first in her discussion of her assigned college roommate who refused to share a room with a "Mexican." Later in the interview when Mari describes a discriminatory encounter at work, she also shifts her terminology. Recall Mari's words as she describes the incident detailed in Chapter Two:

> I felt like one of the parents did not like me because I was Mexican. . . .
> I felt like it was a discrimination thing. But I don't think that the school wanted to hear about it. And I felt very strongly that it was because I was Mexican and I don't deny it. And that is the thing—that I don't make it a quiet thing.

Mari did not feel that in either of these episodes she was mistaken for an immigrant. Her assigned roommate knew that she was a fellow college student from Texas. At work, both her colleagues and her students' parents also typically know that she is from the United States, speaks unaccented English, and is college educated. Thus, it is not that in these moments she is assumed to be an immigrant and hence describes herself as being perceived as "Mexican" in terms of her nationality. Rather, for Mari and other respondents who shift to identifying as "Mexican" when discussing discriminatory episodes, two processes appear to be at play in these moments.

First, discrimination is often described by Mexican Americans in the study as something that occurs due to being "Mexican." This is the case even when the perpetrator knows the person is not an immigrant. Mexicanness is tied to stigma, while Americanness remains linked to privilege and acceptance.[3] Hence, "American" drops off their identification in these moments where they encounter discrimination. This resonates with themes discussed in Chapter Two where respondents who identified strongly as "American" would minimize their experiences with racism. If being American means inclusion, then detailing accounts of exclusion one faces is not congruent with that identity.

Second, when encountering prejudice, many interviewees respond by countering with expressions of pride in their Mexican heritage, and this can manifest in a switch to using the label "Mexican" in that situation. This was illustrated in the accounts of "other race" respondents in Chapter Three. But here we see how self-identified "white" Mexican Americans like Mari may also use expressions of pride in the face of discrimination in the stories they tell about such incidents. Mari explains that she is "Mexican" and "doesn't deny it." While she identifies as "white" on the census and emphasizes her Americanness in her interactions with others, her label-choice shifts in her stories of discrimination. This reveals at least a momentary digression from her discomfort with conflating her identity with that of immigrants. She is a "Mexican" when confronted with racism.

Mike Vargas uses assertions of Mexicanness in a similar fashion. He typically identifies as "Hispanic" both formally and in daily life, defining the term as someone of Mexican ancestry who was born in the United States. At a party he attended a few years ago, someone made offensive remarks regarding "Mexicans." Mike describes how he immediately responded by stating firmly that he is "Mexican." "And I never call myself that," he explains. The woman responded that she was referring to immigrants and not "Hispanics" like Mike. Yet, in that instance, Mike insisted that he too was a "Mexican." For Mike, this use of "Mexican" implies an alliance with Mexican immigrants.

Very few Mexican Americans in the study commonly refer to themselves as "Mexican" as a primary identifier. One such person is Juliana Sanchez, discussed in Chapter Three, who occupies the most extreme point on the anti-racist end of the racial ideology continuum: Racism is endemic. Regarding her racial selection on the census, she says: "I would put Mexican. I'm very proud of my race. I am Mexican. I do not want to be called Spanish or Hispanic or anything else." Juliana went on to discuss her strong support of immigrant rights, explaining that as a bilingual educator she spent many years teaching migrant children. She laments that Mexican Americans often separate themselves from immigrants, expressing her desire that both groups work together and with African Americans to fight for social justice. Her identification as "Mexican" expresses her desire to forge alliances with immigrants.

Overall, with few exceptions, Mexican Americans typically do not identify with the term "Mexican," citing that they are not immigrants. For many, this is stated as a simple categorical difference (e.g., "I was born here. I am not an immigrant, and therefore I am not a Mexican."). Others, particularly on the "white" end of the ideological spectrum, strongly refute the label in attempts to distance themselves from immigrants and mark themselves as "American." Tension between Mexican Americans and Mexican immigrants further contributes to this process, as interviewees note the lack of acceptance they feel from Mexican immigrants who question their Mexicanness. Most importantly, Mexican Americans' emphatic rejection of the term "Mexican" is related to Anglos' frequent lumping of all persons of Mexican origin into the immigrant category. Mexican Americans resent this denial of their family history, of their American identities. But while Mexican Americans state, at times quite adamantly, that they are not "Mexican," identification with the label surfaces intermittently when they discuss discrimination they face and when they align themselves with immigrants. The next section further addresses the contextual nature of labeling for Mexican Americans, focusing on the role of language.

"Only when I'm speaking Spanish": Identity Labels That Shift in Translation

When asked about the term "Mexicano/a," many Mexican Americans defined the term as synonymous with its English equivalent: "Mexican." That is, they described a Mexicano/a as someone born in Mexico or who lives in Mexico. U.S.-born respondents did not typically use the term "Mexicano/a" as a primary or secondary identifier. Overall, it is immigrants who use this label as a self-referent. However, many Mexican Americans do note that they use the term "Mexicano/a" to describe themselves and other U.S.-born Mexican Americans when they are speaking in Spanish with co-ethnics. The use of Mexicano/a when speaking Spanish *entre nosotros* (among ourselves) implies a change of audience. Among members of one's community there may be less desire to assert Americanness than when one is interacting with Anglos. Hence, much like the use of the label "Mexican" as a way to align themselves with immigrants, Mexican Americans' identification as Mexicano/a also serves this purpose.

Yet, while the terms "Mexican" and "Mexicano/a" can similarly function in this way, the reactions that these words evoke from my interviewees are quite different. When I ask Mexican Americans, "Are you Mexican?" the answer is typically an unwavering and adamant "No." But the word "Mexicano/a" does not elicit the same strong negative reaction. Even though both terms are often defined synonymously by Mexican Americans, their implicit meanings are not the same. In fact, some interviewees even define these labels differently. Tomás Sandoval, an administrative assistant in Mission, explains, "A Mexican I would say is someone from south of the border, . . . but Mexicano could be someone here in the valley." For Tomás, there is a geographic specificity attached to the term "Mexicano" that he connects to persons of Mexican origin in the

Rio Grande Valley. Hence, here, we see the terms "Mexican" and "Mexicano" used to speak of different populations in terms of location vis-à-vis the U.S.-Mexico border. Moreover, ironically, it is the Spanish version of the word that denotes the U.S. side of the border. Indeed, "Mexicano" is more palatable for Mexican Americans in the United States precisely because it is not used by Anglos to label persons of Mexican origin. Thus, the emotionally charged experience of being mistaken for an immigrant, or having racist remarks made in one's presence, is not linked to the term "Mexicano" as it is to the term's English counterpart.

Another label that shifts in meaning from English to Spanish is "Texan/Tejano." Most U.S.-born and immigrant respondents identify both terms as meaning someone from Texas, and Mexican Americans in the study usually do identify as "Texans." Still, the overwhelming majority do not typically use "Tejano/a" to describe themselves, but rather use the label to refer to a particular genre of music. As Ana Solis, a beautician in Del Rio, notes, "When I think Tejano or Tejana, I think of the music."

However, Mexican Americans frequently acknowledge that they use "Tejano/a" in one specific context: when saying where they are from in Spanish conversation. Irene Hernandez comments:

Tejano, because I am from Texas and really the name of the state was Tejas, so yes I am a Tejana. *Si estoy hablando español, soy tejana* [if I am speaking Spanish, I am Tejana]. I wouldn't say, *Yo soy de* Texas [I am from Texas]. That would be idiotic. *Yo soy tejana, yo soy de Tejas*, if I were speaking Spanish.

Irene and many others remarked that the use of "Tejano/a" to signify their place of origin when speaking Spanish is simply easier and less awkward than using "Texan." But like the use of "Mexicano," "Tejano" evokes very different meanings than its English translation. In particular, there is a lower-class association with both Tejano music and the label itself. Furthermore, for some, Tejano is geographically tied to certain areas along the Texas-Mexico border and their particular linguistic style. Martha Mendoza, an interviewee from Del Rio, explains:

I am a Texan, but I don't like to consider myself just a Texan. I like to consider myself—I don't know. To me a Tejano or a Tejana is the people more that live down in the [Rio Grande] Valley, they have a low profile, a lower esteem or a lower education, that speak the Tex-Mex language. Because I don't feel, me myself, I have been told by many people that I don't speak the Tex-Mex language. I speak a higher level of Spanish and English. My daddy was very strict on that. . . . He tried to teach us good Spanish and at home we'd always speak Spanish, we wouldn't speak English. . . . He said, "English you can learn it in school. . . . Spanish you'll learn it at home," so we used—he was very strict about teaching us a very correct Spanish.

Martha's and others' linking the word "Tejano" to persons who are from the Rio Grande Valley further led to less identification with the term for many Mexican Americans who feel they do not identify with this regional identity.

My findings with regard to the linguistic context of these labels reveal how terms that may be literal translations are not in fact synonymous in their meanings. "Texan" does not carry with it the association with a working-class identity or specific styles of music like "Tejano/a" does. Moreover, for Mexican Americans, "Mexicano" does not have the same offensive quality as "Mexican" because it is not used by Anglos but, rather, by persons of Mexican origin to refer to themselves. The next section further details how Mexican Americans and Mexican immigrants define and utilize labels in differing way, exposing the divergent ways in which identity is constructed relationally for both groups.

Contrasting Uses of Panethnic Labels for Mexican Americans and Mexican Immigrants

As previously discussed, the labels "Latino" and "Hispanic" have been found to emerge in the narratives of Latinos when they assert "racial" similarity in terms of how they are treated by others (Padilla 1985; De Genova and Ramos-Zayas 2003). Research also notes how these panethnic identities can further be evoked by Latinos as a way of differentiating themselves from other Latino national-origin groups (Valdez 2011). However, while previous research has explored the differing ways in which "Hispanic" and "Latino" are used as either uniting or dividing labels for Latinos, very little scholarship qualitatively explores how the terms "Hispanic" and "Latino" are defined and utilized in divergent ways or how their uses can vary within national-origin groups themselves. My interviews reveal that Mexican Americans assign very different meanings to "Hispanic" vs. "Latino" and that neither truly represents a panethnic label for them. In contrast, Mexican immigrants use "Hispanic" and "Latino" more interchangeably to denote Spanish speakers and often employ the term "Hispanic" when discussing how they are classified and racialized in a U.S. context.

While the definitions immigrants and Mexican Americans attach to these terms differ, the meanings both groups assign these labels are highly dependent, constructed in relation to each other. Indeed, Mexican Americans use "Hispanic" specifically to distinguish themselves from immigrants. Ruben Perez, introduced in Chapter Two, provides a perfect example of this. Ruben lives in Mission, Texas, where he works at a nearby library. Recall how Ruben described his recent stint living in the Midwest, detailing the contrast between how he was treated there compared with his home state. Ruben explains, "I find myself down here defending myself more as not being Mexican. [And I say] 'I'm not a Mexican, I'm a Hispanic.'" Ruben is frequently profiled and searched at immigration checkpoints each time he leaves South Texas on trips to San Antonio or Austin. This leaves him feeling defensive about his identity as an American citizen. Hence, he uses "Hispanic" to mark himself as from the United States. Mexican Americans in the study generally characterize "Hispanic" as referring to U.S.-born persons of Mexican origin. Moreover, those Mexican Americans who define the term "Hispanic" as pertaining more generally to Spanish speakers in the United States still overwhelmingly employ the label as a way to distinguish themselves from Mexican immigrants. A conversation with one of my key informants in Del Rio, Texas, further illustrates this usage. When I asked what locations in town would be the best places to find immigrant interviewees for the study, she responded, "Oh, you want immigrants too. I thought you were just interviewing Hispanics." Overall, "Hispanic" was continually characterized by my Mexican American respondents as "what we call ourselves here," with "we" referring specifically to Mexican-origin persons born in the United States.

In stark contrast, the term "Latino" was typically defined by Mexican Americans as a label describing those "not from here in the United States" and "not of Mexican origin." While most were certain that the word did not describe them, many Mexican Americans often expressed uncertainty as to what specific groups "Latino" would describe. For example, Cristina Garza is a teacher in Del Rio, introduced in Chapter Three. When asked, "Who is Latino?" she responds:

> Somebody Latino or Latina would probably be somebody from [*long pause, as she is thinking*] . . . from Latin Mexico [*laughing*]. I don't know who that would be. Would it be Cubans? No, because [in] Cuba, they

would be Cubans. And I have a cousin who married a guy from Colombia. He's Colombiano. He doesn't consider himself Latino. That's a good question. I don't know who that describes.

Mexican Americans in the study generally define "Latinos" as people either from or living in some other non-Mexican Latin American country. Most associate the term with South America and/or Central America: "Everyone south of Mexico." Diana Espinosa, a nurse in McAllen, defines "Latino" as describing someone "probably like in Ecuador or somewhere over there, you know, but not here. Hispanic is the majority of our culture here." Others mentioned Puerto Ricans or Cubans. For example, my conversation with Marco Valdez, the third-generation Mexican American in Mission, went as follows:

> Marco: A Latino would probably be somebody from any Latin country, be it Cuba, be it South America, or anybody that speaks the Spanish or the Latin language.
>
> JAD: Would you label as Latino?
>
> Marco: No, I would label [someone] Latino if they are not Hispanic. Hispanic I am assuming that—I'm taking that to be Mexican—you know Hispanic, you know that speaks Spanish.

Marco's remarks here demonstrate how even when both "Hispanic" and "Latino" are defined as referring to those who speak Spanish, their implicit meanings are very different. Marco associates "Latino" with the Caribbean and South America, while "Hispanic" is used to describe persons of Mexican origin. Moreover, although here Marco uses "Hispanic" to describe Mexicans generally, earlier in the interview he defined Hispanic as being of Mexican heritage but "born in the United States."

In addition to identifying "Latino" as pertaining to persons from non-Mexican, Latin American countries, Mexican Americans often associate "Latino" with media figures, especially singers. "When you say Latino I think of the music, of singers" was a common refrain. My interviewees further associate the label with "what they call us on television." That is, they view the term as something put on "Hispanics" by the media. Del Rio resident Ana Solis explains, "Latino or Latina. It comes to mind somebody I see on TV like Jennifer Lopez, or some guy that is maybe Puerto Rican or something else." Mexican Americans comment in particular that while they have heard or seen the word on television, they do not use it to describe themselves.

The association of "Latino" with famous people on television also creates a higher-class and lighter-skinned image that some Mexican Americans link to the label "Latino." Matt Chavez, a retired administrative assistant in Del Rio, dislikes the word "Latino" precisely because he feels it applies to elite or more European-origin persons. Matt says:

> Latin. I don't know where they get the Latino because there's no Latin in us. I don't know what that means. Do you watch those Mexican *novelas* [soap operas]? . . . Most of the people in them, they are all white people. You tell me why? Where are the Mexican people from Mexico? Where are the Indians? Where are the half-breeds? It tells me one thing—that Mexico is a country more or less like the United States. Because the Europeans that invaded Mexico, they remained in Mexico. They are the rich people with the French names. And the other groups, the Spanish people that came . . . so those are the people that I guess you could really call Latinos in the sense that they have very little Indian blood.

Matt's comments further emphasize the term "Latino" as disconnected from the lives of Mexican Americans, as for him it denotes privilege. Notice that Matt refers to people in Spanish-language soap operas, connecting the term to media images and particularly ones that fail to represent Mexican-origin people accurately. Finally, a few Mexican Americans who had traveled in the United States (some as migrant workers) are aware that "Latino" is a term that is commonly used in other parts of the country, particularly in California. Robert Jiménez, a police officer in McAllen, says, "I think of Californians. Hispanic people in California label themselves as Latinos." Overall, most Mexican American respondents describe "Latino" as referring to someone who is a non-Mexican Spanish speaker, a famous person on television or in music, and/or a "Hispanic" person who does not live in Texas.

For Mexican immigrants, the meanings and uses of both "Latino" and "Hispanic" are quite different from Mexican Americans. First, as highlighted in the preceding chapter, Mexican immigrants in the study primarily identify as Mexicano/a. When "Hispanic" does emerge in the narratives of immigrants, it is in stories of discrimination they encounter in the United States. Recall how Pablo Ceballos, a restaurant manager in the Dallas area, described how he faces discrimination for being "Hispanic" in the United States. Many others commented on how "Hispanics" are treated here, referring to both U.S.-born and immigrant Latinos. Thus, for immigrants, "Hispanic" emerges as a term that unites them with Mexican Americans and other Spanish speakers in the United States, expressing their shared heritage and struggles with discrimination.

This usage directly contrasts with how Mexican Americans use "Hispanic" to distinguish themselves from immigrants. Moreover, as discussed earlier in the chapter, Mexican Americans use "Mexican" to refer to themselves when recounting racist encounters. Immigrants, however, define both "Mexican" and "Mexicano/a" synonymously as solely describing persons born in Mexico. This exclusivity is sometimes evoked specifically when immigrants distance themselves from Mexican Americans, stating that only they are "Mexicanos/as." Recall how Alma Fuentes in the preceding chapter was heavily invested in distinguishing herself and her children from Mexican Americans, believing stereotypes that Mexican Americans are lazy and less industrious.

Marisol Ruiz, a middle-class Mexican immigrant also discussed in the previous chapter, explains her perspective on various labels:

> I am Mexicana because I was born in Mexico. You are Mexico-Americana because you were born here. We are Latinas, the two of us. We are Hispanas, the two of us. We are Latinas because Spanish is a Latin language. We are Hispanas because we have Spanish heritage.

Marisol tells me that we are both Latinas and Hispanas but that only she is Mexicana. Her remarks here are emblematic of how most immigrants in the study define these terms. Hence, the very labels Mexican Americans use to align themselves with immigrants are the same terms that immigrants use to separate themselves from Mexican Americans, and vice versa.

Conclusion

A number of studies have explored labeling preferences among Latinos, and Mexican Americans specifically, including examinations of how Latinos may employ more than one label in their identification (Oboler 1995; Jones-Correa and Leal 1996; Rodríguez 2000; Ochoa 2004). My research illustrates the complexity of label use among Latinos, highlighting the relationship between the use of labels and racial ideology, as respondents shift their identities in specific contexts depending upon to whom they are speaking, in what language, and the goal of the interaction. Additionally, my interviews reveal how label use varies even within the same national-origin group, as Mexican Americans and Mexican immigrants use terms in very different ways.

Nearly all Mexican American and Mexican immigrant respondents report using more than one term to describe themselves. The primary influence in label choice for both groups hinges on how they position themselves relative to each other in a given moment. Labels can either affirm connections between Mexican Americans and immigrants or separate them. Those Mexican Americans on the "white" side of the racial ideology continuum are most invested in distinguishing themselves from immigrants, in line with their politics of aligning with a white American identity as a defensive strategy.

This process of identity negotiation is embedded in a larger social structure that is characterized by the white racial frame (Feagin 2010). Both Mexican Americans and Mexican immigrants respond to the ways in which they are devalued in society, often internalizing negative images about themselves and each other. This process makes their situational and fluid use of labels vastly different from situational ethnicity among European Americans, as fluidity in label choice is in part a function of the racialization and discrimination they face. Both groups are attempting to manage stigma through their ideological response and corresponding label choice by either adopting distancing maneuvers or identifying in solidarity with each other.

CHAPTER 6

Re-envisioning Our Understanding
of Latino Racial Identity

Nonetheless, race is still real; it still exists. We may question its necessity, the right of anyone to establish such markers, and its validity as a scientific concept. We may see it as unjust and want to change it. But we must acknowledge its significance in our lives. It can be deconstructed, but it cannot be dismissed.
CLARA E. RODRÍGUEZ, *CHANGING RACE*

. . . there are at least two concepts, rather than one, that are vitally necessary to the understanding of Latina/o identity in the United States: ethnicity and race. Using only ethnicity belies the reality of most Latinas/os' everyday experiences, as well as obscures our own awareness about how ethnic identifications often do the work of race while seeming to be theoretically correct and politically advanced. Race dogs our steps; let us not run from it lest we cause it to increase its determination.
LINDA MARTÍN ALCOFF, "IS LATINA/O IDENTITY A RACIAL IDENTITY?"

At a conference I attended a few years ago, an audience member posed a provocative question to a panel on racial identities. "Why are you talking about Latinos as a racial minority group when they are white?" he asked. He continued, "Most of them check white for their race on the census." A very lively and productive exchange followed. Panelists explained how according to the census, Latino/Hispanic is not a "race," but rather a panethnic category composed of persons who may be of any "race." Moreover, they explained how while it is true that approximately half of Latinos do identify as "white" on the census, a substantial number also identify as "other race" and write in a Latino identifier.

The commentary that followed was largely focused on the idea that differences in skin color may lead to divergent experiences with racialization, and hence a variety of racial responses on the census. Audience members further remarked on how acculturation might affect labeling practices such that later-generation Latinos might be more assimilated and thus more likely to identify as racially white. The arguments and examples that emerged in the discussion reveal common assumptions about what whiteness means: that it is an indicator of lighter skin color, cultural assimilation, and integration.

Indeed, Latino racial responses on the census have typically been interpreted in exactly this way.[1] For example, using national census data, Tafoya (2004) examined differences in nativity and socioeconomic status between "white" and "other race" Latinos. While Tafoya acknowledges that other factors, including regional politics, may be at play in the process of racial selection for Latinos,[2] the emphasis of her report, titled "Shades of Belonging," is that Latino racial identification on the census can be interpreted as a proxy for inclusion: the understanding being that those who identify as "white" are indeed accepted as white, while those who indicate "other race" feel less of a sense of belonging or acceptance with regard to the dominant society.

Tafoya does not believe that these differences in levels of "belonging" are based solely on skin color or that the fact that many Latinos identify as "white" means that race is unimportant or irrelevant in their lives. However, much like the audience member who posed the question to the conference panel, some social scientists have indeed interpreted Latino racial identification in these ways (Patterson 2001; Yancey 2003). Citing the substantial number of Latinos who identify as white on the census, some scholars have argued that Latinos should not be considered a "racial" minority group at all but, rather, a white ethnic group on the path toward full assimilation like European immigrants of the past (Patterson 2001; Yancey 2003). Yancey (2003), for example, bases his argument that Latinos are for all intents and purposes racially white on the proportion of Latinos who identify as white on the census and on survey data that suggest Latinos exhibit color-blind ideology in their lack of desire to talk about race.

These arguments, however, are largely predicated on an understanding of whiteness and color-blind ideology as they apply to a European American experience. Historically, the construction of whiteness for European Americans evolved from shared skin color, cultural and structural assimilation, and the development of an ideological stance that included the denigration of blackness and other racial minorities (Roediger 1991; Ignatiev 1995; Hale 1998; Feagin 2010). Moreover, color-blind ideology among European Americans is integrally linked to racial privilege, as membership in the dominant racial majority allows for the ability to see oneself as "raceless" and discount the relevance of race in the lives of others (Gallagher 2003; Bonilla-Silva 2010).

But do whiteness and color-blind ideology hold the same meanings for Latinos that they do for European Americans? Do "white" Latinos feel they "belong," while racial "others" exist in the margins of society? What drives decisions regarding Latino racial labeling practices both formally and in daily life? Focusing specifically on Mexican Americans and Mexican immigrants, I began this book with these central questions in mind. My focus throughout the book has been on the disconnect between public and private articulations of race, the meanings of whiteness and racial "otherness" for both Mexican Americans and Mexican immigrants, and the juxtaposition of the constraints of racialization alongside the fluidity of racial and ethnic self-labeling in these communities.

Overall, my findings on the meanings and motivations behind racial self-identification challenge common assumptions in the field, contesting arguments that these formal racial responses are reflective of differences in skin color, divergent levels of assimilation and acculturation, or both. I find that Mexican Americans and Mexican immigrants who label as racially "white" on the census typically identify strongly with their cultural heritage, describe incidents of discrimination, and are not lighter skinned than those who identify as "other race." In fact, some of the darkest-skinned respondents in the study identify as racially "white," and "white" interviewees often relayed some of the most painful stories of discrimination.[3] Yet, while whiteness is not a reflection of color, acceptance, or assimilation for either Mexican Americans or Mexican immigrants, these groups differ substantially from each other in their approach to racial classification.

For Mexican Americans, the most salient factor in determining their racial choices is how they frame their experiences with racialization through the use of discursive strategies. I developed a theoretical framework to explain this process: the racial ideology continuum. On one end of the continuum, mirroring the dominant discourse of American meritocracy, "white" Mexican Americans frequently employ a discursive framework that reflects color-blind racial ideology. They often minimize or deflect the role of race in their lives. There are crucial differences, however, between the uses and motivations behind how Mexican Americans employ color-blind ideology and the ways in which this framework is evoked by European Americans who claim not to "see" race. As targets of racism, Mexican Americans are actually very cognizant of race, and their own stories of discrimination continually contradict their efforts to downplay the significance of race in their lives.

The overwhelming majority of "white" Mexican Americans would, in fact, never use the term "white" as a self-referent outside the context of the census form, and they note that others do not classify them in this way. Rather, whiteness is an identity that Mexican Americans assert publicly with outsiders that emphasizes their "American" identities. This identification embodies an approach intended to combat racial discrimination by emphasizing their similarity to the dominant racial majority. In their efforts to become accepted as "American," Mexican Americans adopt both the racial identification and ideology of the dominant group, including distancing themselves from both African Americans and Mexican immigrants. This explains the prevalence of "white" identification along the Texas-Mexico border, where Mexican Americans find themselves under more scrutiny, as they are confronted with assumptions that they are "Mexican" and not "American."

Mexican Americans historically used the strategy of claiming whiteness to combat segregation throughout the first half of the century (Foley 1998; Gómez 2007). When identifying their race on the census, older respondents often relied on this history, evoking the "official" designation of Mexican Americans as racially white. To project an "American" identity, "white" Mexican Americans also continually downplay their own experiences with discrimination. However, these efforts to fit within the bounds of whiteness have not been successful for my respondents, as most report incidents of racial profiling and discrimination. Thus, it is racial discrimination and not racial privilege that motivates identification with whiteness for Mexican Americans in the study, making their use of both whiteness and color-blind ideology fundamentally different from that of European Americans.

"Other race" respondents occupy the opposite end of the racial ideology continuum. These Mexican Americans speak more openly about the impact of race in their lives, and some articulate strong anti-racist ideologies or counter-frames. As is the case with "white" respondents, discrimination is key to how "other race" Mexican Americans assert their racial identities. While Mexican Americans on this side of the spectrum often cite cultural heritage as an important component in their decision to write in an "other race" response, their experiences with differential treatment are critical to how and why they assert this cultural difference from the dominant majority. Assertions of cultural pride often serve as a "counter-frame," a way of resisting the dominant "white racial frame" (Feagin 2010). While "other race" interviewees do not report greater incidents of discrimination than "white" Mexican Americans, they respond differently to these experiences. Rather than aligning themselves with whiteness, they assert pride in their cultural heritage. Moreover, whereas those who label as "white" construct a firm boundary between themselves and African Americans, "other race" interviewees situate themselves either between whites and African Americans or alongside African Americans. "Other race" respondents are also far more likely to align themselves with immigrants. Overall, my findings with regard to Mexican Americans highlight the critical role of racial ideology in the labeling process, particularly emphasizing the connection between the discursive frameworks my respondents use to talk about their experiences with discrimination and their racial choices.

For Mexican immigrants, assertions of racial identity are also informed by racial ideology. However, immigrants approach racial classification in the United States from a fundamentally different vantage point than do Mexican Americans, as they rely on ideology and constructions of race derived from Mexico. The dominant racial discourse in Mexico is based on an understanding of Mexicans as a mestizo people composed of a melding of Spanish and Indian heritage. While there are indigenous and Afro-origin populations in Mexico, their presence is often left out of Mexico's dominant mestizo racial narrative (Doremus 2001; Sue 2013). Overall, immigrants in the study typically understood their "*raza*" in terms of their national origin as "Mexicanos/as." Those who write in "Hispanic" for their race on the census do so because they understand that this is their assigned identity in the United States. Most do not use the label to self-identify in daily life. Moreover, those who select "white" or "*blanco/a*" for their race are not expressing feelings of inclusion, acculturation, or the adoption of American identities. Rather, for most, identification as either "white" or "Hispanic" reflects efforts to indicate the "correct" answer on the form, as immigrants confront a racial classification system that is foreign to them. As well, some higher-status migrants positioned themselves as racially different from low-income Mexican immigrants, Mexican Americans, and African Americans in their efforts to distance themselves from racial stigma. Overall, my findings resonate with scholarship on racial labeling, which contends that while immigrants acquire new ways of thinking about race in a U.S. context, these identifications do not replace previous racial schemas, but rather become part of a constellation or repertoire of identities they may draw upon (Jones-Correa and Leal 1996; Roth 2012).

Indeed, most Mexican Americans and Mexican immigrants use an array of labels to describe themselves. While the primary distinction I explore in the book is between formal and everyday labeling, interviewees' stories of how and when they use specific terms reveal the influence of racial ideology in how they assert racial identities in daily life as well. For Mexican immigrants and Mexican Americans, racial identification is constructed relationally, as these groups use specific labels to either differentiate themselves from each other or align themselves with one another. This frequently results in the use of various labels in different contexts dependent upon to whom they are speaking, in what language, and the goal of the interaction. For example, recall how Mexican Americans on the "white"/color-blind side of the ideology continuum are most adamant in their rejection of the label "Mexican." Nevertheless, they and other Mexican Americans across the ideological spectrum do refer to themselves as "Mexican" when discussing discrimination they face. Moreover, some adopt the label strategically when confronted with racism. Thus, labeling for Mexican Americans is often fluid, situational, and dependent on context.

Situational ethnic identification is typically associated with European Americans, for whom ethnic identification is self-asserted, optional, and voluntary (Waters 1990). I find, however, that just as the meanings and uses of whiteness and color-blind ideology among Mexican Americans and immigrants differ from those of European Americans, so too does the practice of "situational" racial/ethnic labeling. Unlike European Americans, fluidity in label choice does not mean that racial identification is flexible, optional, or costless for persons of Mexican origin in Texas.[4] Rather, the situational use of labels for both Mexican Americans and immigrants often reflects strategies for dealing with discrimination, as these groups either attempt to avoid stigma through distancing maneuvers or align themselves with each other strategically. Overall, the complex and situational identification of Mexican Americans and Mexican immigrants highlights discrimination and racial ideology as critical factors influencing racial identification for this population both formally and in daily life.

Reconceptualizing Our Understanding of Latinos and the Question of Race

Mexican Americans and other Latinos constitute a large and growing segment of U.S. society, and much contemporary sociological inquiry has focused on how increases in the Latino population affect the racial landscape of the nation. Some scholars hypothesize that Latinos are racially white or are on the path toward assimilating into the white majority (Patterson 2001; Yancey 2003). Others argue that Latinos are not achieving full integration, either due to their own voluntary refusal (Huntington 2004) or as a result of racialization and exclusion (Telles and Ortiz 2008). Still others posit that a racialization process is occurring, whereby depending upon skin color and socioeconomic position, some Latinos will become racialized as white and others as nonwhite (Bonilla-Silva 2004; Golash-Boza 2006; Golash-Boza and Darity 2008; Frank et al. 2010). Much research in this area utilizes quantitative analysis of national surveys, focusing on Latino identification as "white" either on the census or on questionnaires using a similar format (Yancey 2003; Tafoya 2004; Frank et al. 2010).

Examining the degree to which formal identification actually corresponds to lived experiences with race, my interviews with Mexican Americans and Mexican immigrants in multiple Texas communities reveal that racialization and discrimination are still quite pervasive in the lives of both "white" and "other race" respondents. This is not to say that all Mexican Americans and Mexican immigrants in the study experience racialization in the exact same way. As detailed in the narratives of my respondents, factors such as age, generation, location, class background, skin color, and experiences with external classification radically shape racial ideology, influencing racial identification. Yet, across the class and color spectrum, stories of discrimination persist.

Indeed, while some of my interviewees have achieved structural assimilation through acquiring a middle-class status, they still face discrimination in their daily lives as they confront stereotypes that they are lower income, immigrants, or both simply because of their skin color or surname. This resonates with O'Brien's (2008) study of middle-class Latinos and Asian Americans in which she finds that most still face issues with discrimination and racialization despite their economic privilege. Moreover, Vasquez (2011) also notes the persistence of race among middle-class Mexican American families in her study. She terms this phenomenon "racialization despite assimilation."

Similarly, as illustrated by numerous stories throughout the book, race continues to be salient for my respondents, even among those who have surpassed social class barriers. One such poignant example is Ruben Perez, who is frequently detained at border checkpoints in South Texas. Ruben just completed his master's degree and is professionally employed. Moreover, his mother's family dates back many generations in Texas. Still, Ruben studies his facial features in the mirror wondering what makes him seem so "un-American." In marking "white" on the census, Ruben does not express a sense of belonging but, rather, a desire to achieve such acceptance and inclusion. I argue that in light of stories like Ruben's and many others presented in this book, it is imperative that social scientists reconceptualize how we understand Latino racial identification and particularly how we interpret assertions of whiteness. Below, I have outlined three interventions toward this end.

Separating the Personal from the Formal

A number of studies have documented the ways in which Mexican Americans have historically courted whiteness, using such arguments to combat segregation and discrimination (Foley 1998, 2006; Marquez 2003; Gómez 2007; Orozco 2009). These identity claims represent public identities that often did not correspond to how these individuals actually labeled themselves within their own communities (Orozco 2009). Yet, despite this history, contemporary assertions of whiteness on forms such as the census are often taken at face value. Without research to challenge this interpretation, the dominant explanatory narrative remains that whiteness for Mexican Americans and other Latinos represents what it has for European Americans: integration and assimilation. In this book, I have demonstrated how this is not the case for Mexican Americans in the study. Rather, a legacy of the strategic use of whiteness, combined with contemporary color-blind ideology, strongly informs their decisions to identify as racially "white" on the census, a public expression of racial group membership that does not resonate with their personal identification in daily life.

As my interviews highlight, when one asserts a racial label, there is always an audience involved, and how one chooses to identify is dependent upon one's relationship with that audience. This is true not just of interpersonal expressions of racial group membership but of formal ones as well. As Maria Lopez, introduced in Chapter Four, sits at her kitchen table, filling out her census form, she is mindful of her audience: "The form belongs to the U.S. government, and here we are Hispanics." Thus, filling out a question about racial identity does not just reflect how a person sees herself but how she believes the inquirer sees her or how she would like to be seen. This does not mean that formal racial labels are inherently invalid. It simply highlights that all self-labeling is contextual and must be examined and interpreted in this way. I argue that it is especially critical to be mindful of this issue when the audience involved is outside one's community and particularly when the inquirer is an institution of authority such as the federal government. For example, recall how Eddie Martinez, introduced at the outset of the book, identified as "white" because he felt obligated to follow the law, referring to the historical legal definition of Mexican Americans as racially white. Overall, the stories of my respondents challenge social scientists not to conflate formal racial labeling with personal identification, as, for many of my interviewees, there is a disconnect between these identities.

On Talking and Not Talking About Race

As previously stated, some scholars have interpreted survey research indicating that Latinos are less interested in talking about race to mean that they espouse a color-blind ideology that resembles that of European Americans (Yancey 2003). However, while research reveals that European Americans avoid discussing race because they fail to recognize their racial privilege or are unwilling to acknowledge it (Gallagher 2003; Bonilla-Silva 2010), for Mexican Americans such discursive tactics originate not from a place of privilege but rather from one of pain. As most respondents have experienced racial prejudice, talking about race means detailing stories of structural and interpersonal victimization, something understandably uncomfortable because it requires one to relive such painful moments.

During the interviews Mexican Americans would often tell me stories about racial segregation, tracking in school, or other types of discrimination that they had experienced. However, later in the interviews, when I asked directly if they had ever faced discrimination or been treated differently because of their racial or ethnic background, they would answer, "No." As discussed earlier, some of this minimizing of encounters with racism occurs as a result of the desire to project a white, "American" identity. That is, for those who identify as racially white, when the reality of their lived experiences with racism does not match this presentation of self, they experience a kind of cognitive dissonance that can be alleviated only by minimizing those moments when they have been treated as nonwhite.

For example, Matt Chavez identifies as "white" on the census despite not being classified or treated as such by others. Matt grew up on the Mexican side of town in the barrio of San Felipe in Del Rio. Early in the interview, he spoke of his experiences:

> We were discriminated [against]. We were the only district in the whole nation that was all Mexicans, even the coordinators at the school. We were totally segregated—all Mexican. I remember when I joined the ser-

vice I was completely lost because I was not familiar with the Anglo culture at all. I was really lost.

While Matt had volunteered this information at the beginning of our interview, later when I asked if he had ever experienced discrimination or been treated differently, he replied, "No, I don't think so. Well, maybe when I was growing up. But mostly I try to get along with all different kinds of people." A number of interviewees engaged in this discursive tactic of highlighting their ability to "get along with others" when responding to this question. The dominant racial paradigm of the United States emphasizes a color-blind meritocratic society in which those who do not succeed fail due to their own deficiencies. Respondents who identify as "white," exhibiting color-blind ideology, have internalized this belief. Hence, to acknowledge how discrimination has had a detrimental impact on them is to admit failure. Instead, they emphasize their individual abilities to overcome or not be bothered by such experiences. Eileen O'Brien (2008) notes such rhetoric among her middle-class Latino and Asian American respondents, cautioning that this minimizing does not represent "denial" but rather is a strategic response to racism. O'Brien (2008: 125–126) writes:

> Already vilified by racist ideology for being "foreign" and "not American," Latinos and Asian Americans would be seen as even more "un-American" by being one of those "complainers" if they actually testified to the persistence of racism in their lives. Thus, far from engaging in a delusional denial dynamic, these respondents are making a prudent choice to attest to the validity of the American dream and refuse to be further characterized as un-American in the eyes of whites.

Similarly, race-minimizing among my respondents is strategic in this way, as for Mexican Americans who identify as "white," acknowledging the imprint of racism in their lives would undermine their claims to whiteness and American identity. In another powerful example, recall Mari Bredahl's story regarding her assigned college roommate who refused to share a room with her. Minimizing the impact of this incident, Mari says, "I mean it didn't bother me that much. I have a lot of self-confidence. Maybe for someone who did not have as much confidence it would bother them." Obviously this is an experience that Mari remembers decades later, and yet given her ideological stance, to acknowledge its impact on her would undermine both her claims to whiteness and American identity.

Even for those on the opposite end of the ideological spectrum, it can be challenging to speak about racism. Sandra Alvarez, a third-generation Mexican American in her early fifties, identifies as racially "Hispanic" and is in the "Racism is significant" position on the racial ideology continuum. Sandra is open about her past involvement with La Raza Unida political party and views race as an important contemporary problem, yet she still struggles to talk to her grandchildren about Del Rio's painful racial history. After she recently took her young grandchildren to the local cemetery to see their ancestors' graves, they had a lot of questions for her, and Sandra found herself anxious and uncomfortable in the conversation. She recalls:

> So I tried to answer as many questions as I could. And then I explained to them the different types of cemeteries that we have here. I said, "This one, *mija*, we started it as all Hispanics." "What do you mean, grandma?" I said, "Well, *mija*, look at our skin. Your dad is Mexican American. We're Hispanics because we were born here in the United States. And this cemetery was for Hispanic Americans. And there's another cemetery that started out for the Anglos." "But why, grandma?" And I'm going like, "What did I get into?"

Sandra struggled to explain the history of segregation in Del Rio to her eight- and six-year-old granddaughters, and she dreads the continuing questions about race that will likely emerge in the coming years. Several interviewees like Sandra spoke of not wanting to frighten or embitter children and grandchildren with such stories. Thus, not talking about race can also be an attempt to shelter future generations from these episodes.[5]

In sum, I find the reasons Mexican Americans downplay discrimination and avoid talking about race are rooted in a completely different set of circumstances than what has been documented in the narratives of European Americans. Race-minimizing for Mexican Americans is a defensive strategy that emerges from discrimination. These findings clearly problematize the interpretation of a lack of desire among Latinos to talk about race and discrimination as indicative of racial privilege and assimilation. Rather, the stories of my respondents demonstrate how minimizing discrimination can also be a symptom of experiences with racialization.

Distinguishing Federal Definitions from Regional Constructions of Race

Another important caveat regarding the conceptualization of Latino racial identification that emerges from the study is the disjuncture between federal and regional constructions of race. The federal government defines the categories of "Hispanic" and "Latino" synonymously as pertaining to Spanish-speaking populations and their descendants in the United States (Ennis et al 2011). My interviews reveal that while Mexican immigrants do use these labels in this way, Mexican Americans clearly do not. Rather, Mexican Americans in my research sites use "Hispanic" to describe U.S.-born persons of Mexican ancestry, and they understand "Latino" to mean non-Mexican persons of Latin American descent.

In academia, "Latino" is often thought of as more politically correct than "Hispanic," as it is frequently described as a label that emerged from Latinos themselves. In contrast, "Hispanic" is viewed as a government construct that comes from outside the community (Oboler 1995).[6] Mexican Americans in Texas, however, see "Latino" as a label imposed on them by outsiders (the media) that does not resonate with how they define themselves. On the other hand, they understand "Hispanic" as "what we call ourselves here" in the community. These findings have implications for how we interpret "panethnic" identities, highlighting the need to consider how such terms may be employed in specific communities in ways that vary substantially by region. Hence, "Hispanic" in New York does not necessarily carry the same meaning as "Hispanic" in Florida, Texas, or California. Along the same lines, as Alcoff (2000: 38) notes, Latino "will mean race in California, Texas, New York, and Florida, and perhaps ethnicity only in a few locations." These divergent ways of understanding racial and ethnic constructions regionally make measuring and interpreting both race and Hispanic origin at the federal level a challenge.

On the Measurement of Race: Practical Concerns Amidst a Complex Reality

A few years ago when I presented some of my work on this topic at a conference, I encountered an audience member with some concerns about my project. He thought that in highlighting the disjuncture between the formal and everyday labeling practices of Mexican Americans, I was making an argument against measuring race on the census at all. As someone who uses racial data to study racial disparities and antidiscrimination legislation, he found this a disturbing proposition. I assured him that this is most definitely not my opinion on the matter. My interviews reveal that racism is pervasive in the lives of my respondents. I believe the prevalence of discrimination against racial minorities in the United States necessitates that we measure race, enact laws to protect racial minorities, and enforce such policies. Our ability as social scientists to inform social policy in this way often hinges on acquiring the data needed to demonstrate the continuing significance of racial disparities. Hence, I believe that removing questions of racial identification on federal and local forms would represent a setback in our path toward racial equity. Banishing race from forms will not remedy racism but merely make it more difficult to track discrimination.

Given the problems that I have highlighted with regard to interpretations of Latino racial responses, how should we proceed in asking about race? If Latinos do indeed constitute a racialized minority, should they be listed on the census as a race? Indeed, proposals to transform "Hispanic" into a racial designation on the census have been submitted numerous times over the years (Rodríguez 2000). However, none have been successful thus far. One of the main points evoked in arguments against this proposal is that Latinos include a broad range of phenotypes, or "races" (Rodríguez 2000). While the category of "Hispanic/Latino" is typically associated with a "brown" skin color, there are Latinos who are primarily of European, Asian, or Afro-origin descent and therefore do not fit this image. Hence, if "Hispanic/Latino" is added on the census as a race, how would an Afro-Latino person identify, as black or Latino or both? Moreover, if all Latinos were to be collapsed into one racial category, it would be impossible to measure racial disparities that may exist among Latinos, such as how Afro-Latinos fare compared with other Latinos.

Another very valid concern regarding the proposal to make "Hispanic" a race is the possibility that this would create an undercount because some Latinos may not want to identify themselves as racially distinct from the dominant white majority. While testing various questionnaire formats in the mid-1990s, the U.S. Census Bureau (1997) found that Latinos were less likely to check the "Hispanic/Latino" box when it was listed as a racial option vs. an ethnic one. This resonates with my finding that many Mexican Americans resist being racialized as nonwhite on the census, and reveals the challenges of counting a racialized group in which some members actively resist racial differentiation from the dominant majority.

Moreover, considering the ways in which the census is used for various political purposes, a significant increase in the undercount of Latinos could be detrimental to the community.

Yet having "Hispanic/Latino" listed as an "ethnic" or "origin" group is also problematic because it elides the lived realities of Latinos as they have been and continue to be racialized in the United States. Among my "other race" respondents, many felt that their experiences were unrecognized and invalidated by the government due to the absence of a racial option. Moreover, while my interviewees answered the 2000 Census questionnaire, the latest 2010 Census included additional instructions regarding the questions about Hispanic origin and race that some Latinos found disturbing. The added sentence read: "For this census, Hispanic origins are not races." This controversial statement frustrated many Latinos who, after receiving their 2010 Census, took to the Internet to express dismay regarding being instructed that they are not a "race."[7] Indeed, Gustavo Arellano, author of "Ask a Mexican," a prominent, nationally syndicated column known for its comic political commentary, devoted a special issue to the topic that answered readers' questions. Criticizing the setup of the question, Arellano (2010: 1) wrote, ". . . do we really expect anything right to come out of Washington regarding Mexicans and public policy? Been one disaster after another since 1846." While Arellano expresses humor, his words clearly also indicate distrust and suspicion, drawing on a reference to the violent conquest of the southwestern United States.

Thus, on the one hand, a Hispanic/Latino racial option acknowledges historical and contemporary racialization of Latinos, which can be validating. However, as many Latinos wish to resist racial "othering," listing Hispanic/Latino as a race could make some Latinos refuse to check that box, potentially contributing to an undercount. It is a challenging dilemma, but new evidence from a recent survey conducted by the Census Bureau provides some ideas for a potential solution.

In August 2012, the U.S. Census revealed key findings from the Census 2010 Race and Hispanic Origin Alternative Questionnaire Experiment (AQE). This comprehensive study involved the distribution of experimental census questionnaires to households during the 2010 Census with follow-up telephone interviews with those same respondents to ascertain how well their written response corresponded to the labels they generally use to self-identify (Compton et al. 2012).[8] Over 385,000 households completed the AQE experimental questionnaires, and approximately one-fifth of these respondents were contacted for a phone interview.[9] Additionally the AQE study included focus groups with over 750 participants to investigate how different population groups respond to various questionnaire formats.[10] Seventeen questionnaire designs were utilized in the study. These formats tested a range of issues, including the visual arrangement of racial categories and examples, the wording of the question itself, and, most pertinent to this study, combining the race and Hispanic-origin questions.[11] I have included one example of the latter that has been termed the "streamlined" question (Figure 6.1).

Findings from the AQE revealed no significant undercount in the number of Latinos in any of the combined race and Hispanic-origin questions tested (Compton et al. 2012). These combined questions, such as the one shown in Figure 6.1, asked persons for their "race or origin." This circumvents actually calling Latinos a "race" for those who may resist racialization but also does not separate Latinos or state that they are not a race. In this "streamlined" version, groups that are typically listed as races such as whites and blacks are also given the opportunity to write in an ethnic origin. In the focus groups conducted by the Census Bureau's research team, many respondents expressed that giving all groups the opportunity to identify an origin is both more equitable and respectful (Compton et al. 2012). It does not single out Latinos but rather acknowledges that all "racial" groups are composed of individuals from various ethnic origins, including whites.

Latinos filling out the "streamlined" question can identify solely as Latino (further specifying an origin) or may opt to indicate white or black alone or in addition to marking Latino. For example, an Afro-Cuban individual could check the "Latino/Hispanic" box, the "black" category, or both and write in "Cuban" for his/her origin under either option. Even for non-Latino groups, this format provides the opportunity for groups to better articulate the nuances of their identities. The ability to note that one is racially black and of Haitian origin, for example, might better capture the identity of a Haitian American than the "black or African American" box typically provided.

Moreover, each combined race and Hispanic/Latino-origin questionnaire tested in the study resulted in a dramatic reduction in the number of "other race" responses. In the 2010 Census, nearly 40% of Latinos identified as "other race," making this group the third largest racial category on the census after "white" and "black." The combined-question formats resulted in a decrease in the overall number of "other race" responses to less than 1% (Compton et al. 2012). Moreover, significantly fewer Latinos (an estimated 9–16%) identified as "white" on the combined-question forms, compared with approximately half of Latinos who marked "white"

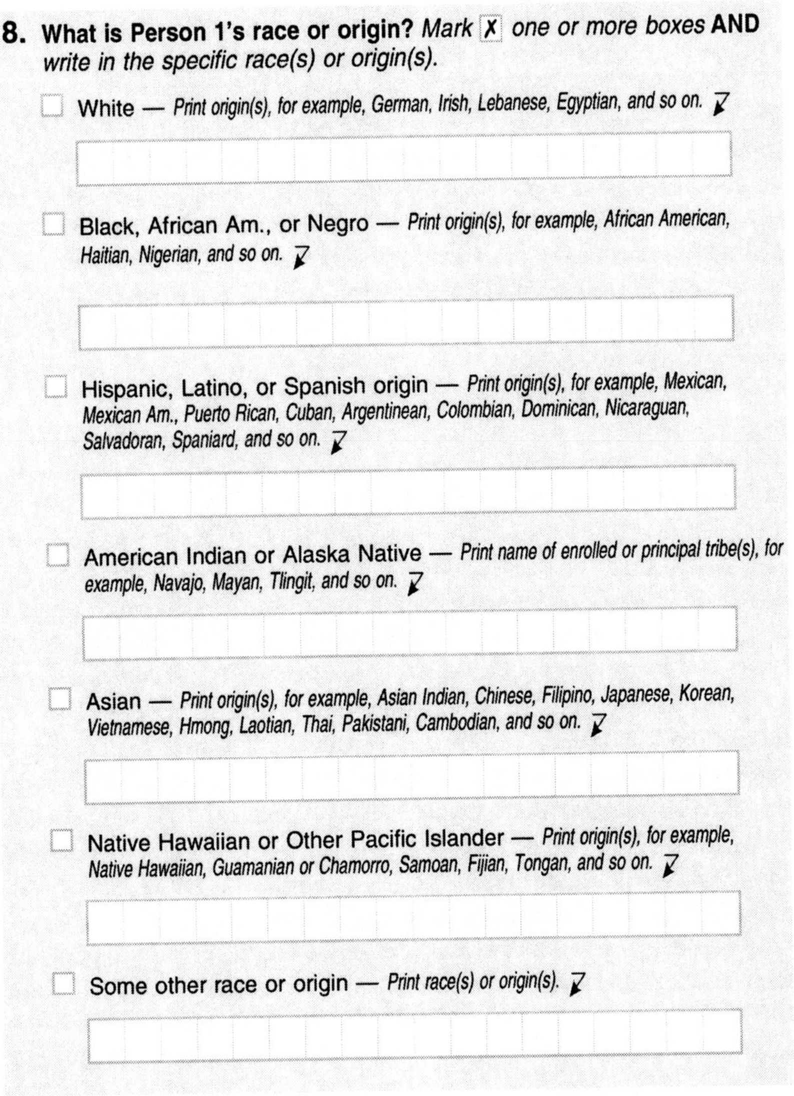

8. What is Person 1's race or origin? Mark ⊠ one or more boxes **AND** *write in the specific race(s) or origin(s).*

☐ White — *Print origin(s), for example, German, Irish, Lebanese, Egyptian, and so on.* ↗

[ ]

☐ Black, African Am., or Negro — *Print origin(s), for example, African American, Haitian, Nigerian, and so on.* ↗

[ ]

☐ Hispanic, Latino, or Spanish origin — *Print origin(s), for example, Mexican, Mexican Am., Puerto Rican, Cuban, Argentinean, Colombian, Dominican, Nicaraguan, Salvadoran, Spaniard, and so on.* ↗

[ ]

☐ American Indian or Alaska Native — *Print name of enrolled or principal tribe(s), for example, Navajo, Mayan, Tlingit, and so on.* ↗

[ ]

☐ Asian — *Print origin(s), for example, Asian Indian, Chinese, Filipino, Japanese, Korean, Vietnamese, Hmong, Laotian, Thai, Pakistani, Cambodian, and so on.* ↗

[ ]

☐ Native Hawaiian or Other Pacific Islander — *Print origin(s), for example, Native Hawaiian, Guamanian or Chamorro, Samoan, Fijian, Tongan, and so on.* ↗

[ ]

☐ Some other race or origin — *Print race(s) or origin(s).* ↗

[ ]

Figure 6.1. "Streamlined" Census 2010 Alternative Questionnaire Experiment (AQE) Sample Form.

for their race in the 2010 Census.[12] Both follow-up interviews and focus groups conducted as a part of the AQE revealed findings similar to my research: Latinos who marked "white" for their race in the standard separate-questions design said that they did not usually identify as such in their daily lives. In contrast, those Latinos who marked "white" in a combined-question format, reported that this corresponded with how they self-identify. Overall, the Census Bureau noted greater consistency in Latino racial reporting in the combined format such that formal racial labeling on the census better matched the actual preferred racial identification as articulated by the same respondents in the telephone reinterview (Compton et al. 2012).

Furthermore, recall the concern that a combined race and Hispanic-origin question would make it more difficult to examine socioeconomic differences among Latinos, such as how Afro-Latinos compare with other Latinos. Importantly, the AQE combined formats did not result in a decrease in the number of Latinos who indicated they there were "black." That is, the number of persons who marked "Latino/Hispanic" and "black" in the combined questions was comparable to the number of Latinos who identified as racially black in the standard separate-questions format.[13]

Given such promising results, I believe the "streamlined" question or one of similar construction represents a viable solution.[14] However, based on the narratives of my respondents, there are a few additional points to consider. First, as being recognized as "American" is very important to many Mexican Americans in the study, I recommend making this more prominent in the examples listed under the Hispanic/Latino-origin option. Currently, "Mexican Am." is listed as an example: it could be spelled out as "American." On a related note, the "Asian" option does not have "American" listed anywhere in the examples. I recommend changing the racial option to "Asian or Asian American" and listing at least one example with "American" in it, such as "Chinese American." Since both Latinos and Asian Americans are often cast as "forever foreigners" (Tuan 1998), and not fully American, this would represent an important gesture of inclusivity.[15]

There is still further testing to be done before a decision for the 2020 Census will be made, but I hope that the Census Bureau will be able to make changes so that the data more accurately reflect the racial and ethnic identification of Latinos and other groups. Finally, regardless of how the issue of formal racial classification for Latinos is eventually resolved, it is critical that social scientists re-envision how Latino racial identification is to be interpreted: not as merely a product of skin color or assimilation but rather as fundamentally connected to racial ideology and responses to racism.

Final Thoughts on Whiteness, Americanness, and the Racial Place of Mexican Americans

Contrary to media images that bombard the American public with fears that Mexican Americans refuse to embrace their American identities (Chavez 2008), I find Mexican Americans in Texas quite invested in their wish to be seen as Americans. Indeed, this desire is so profound that many respondents assert white racial identities in order to present this American identity publicly. Studies of whiteness by George Lipsitz (1998) and David Roediger (2002), among many others, have documented the investment in whiteness for European Americans as an identity that both historically and currently confers power and property rights in the United States. Cheryl Harris (1993) extends this argument, suggesting that whiteness not only confers property but is property itself. Thus, poor whites cling to it, even while not always reaping monetary or property benefits. They hold a tight grip on whiteness as it may be the only property that they do own. One could say that whiteness for Mexican Americans operates similarly: those who identify as "white" cling to whiteness not in spite of but because of their position as a stigmatized group. However, these "white" Mexican Americans are not generally recognized as white by others. Hence, it becomes quite clear that they do not truly "own" whiteness as it is not a validated social identification for them.

Mary Waters (1990) concludes her study of white ethnic identities among multigenerational European Americans by examining a problem she finds in their "optional" ethnicities: her respondents often compared their experiences with flexible and voluntary "ethnic" identities to the experiences of "racial" minorities. That is, these white ethnics frequently minimized or downplayed discrimination in the lives of people of color, generalizing from their own experiences with ethnicity. Waters explains this problem with blurring the line between situational ethnicity and racialized identities as the real "costs of a costless community."

Indeed, a number of my "white" Mexican American respondents made this comparison themselves, likening their own experiences to those of white European Americans, even though their racial realities do not match this. What are the costs of this comparison, of identification with whiteness for Mexican Americans? First, there is a disconnect between "white" Mexican Americans' lived experiences and what they write on the form, which minimizes the historical and contemporary racialization and discrimination in their communities. This has implications for how respondents understand their own identities and how they define their relationships with others. My respondents' identification with whiteness and color-blind ideology creates a wedge between them and others in their communities, as these "white" Mexican Americans distance themselves from other Mexican Americans and from Mexican immigrants. Moreover, claiming whiteness further distances my respondents from African Americans and other racialized populations in the United States, potentially hindering coalitions between these groups. Thus, I argue that while whiteness and color-blind discursive frameworks for my Mexican American respondents are fundamentally different from those of European Americans in both their motivations and uses, the effect of these strategies can be similarly detrimental in undermining efforts to organize against racial injustice. Finally, as these assertions of whiteness are interpreted by so many as a sign of inclusion, Latinos' continuing struggle to be recognized as full and equal Americans is discounted.

Notes on Methodology

Respondents for the study were gathered through a number of sources, including community events and places such as churches, local markets, schools, bingo parlors, and other social gathering spaces. I am personally from the Dallas/Fort Worth area, and my mother was born and raised in Mission. Having long-standing relationships with both these communities, as well as family ties in Del Rio, helped me to establish connections. Beginning with a few key informants, I sought referrals from these individuals. I was cautious to get only one or two names from specific individuals to ensure diversity in terms of gender, age, educational attainment, class background, neighborhood of residence, and generational status. Table A summarizes the key demographics of the eighty-six respondents.

Specifically regarding educational attainment, nine respondents or 10% of the sample had not graduated high school, and twenty-nine had graduated high school or passed the General Educational Development (GED) examination but did not go on to college (34%). Twenty respondents or 23% of the sample had some postsecondary education such as vocational training or junior college, or they had taken some college courses but had not completed a four-year degree. Twenty-eight respondents or 33% of the sample had graduated college.

Twenty-one respondents were Mexican immigrants, while sixty-five were U.S.-born Mexican Americans. Classifying U.S.-born respondents by generational status was complicated because many respondents were from parents or grandparents of different generational statuses. An example of this would be a woman with a mother who was a Mexican immigrant and a father who was a second-generation Mexican American. Throughout the book, I provide such detail about my respondents, but for the purpose of presenting the generational distribution of the sample here, I have simplified them into categories based on the most recent immigrant background. That is, if one parent was an immigrant, I counted that person as second generation. Thirty-seven respondents or 43% of the sample were second-generation Mexican American, born in the United States with at least one immigrant parent. I also interviewed twenty-eight respondents (33%) who were third generation or beyond, born in the United States of U.S.-born parents. I should also note 84 of the 86 respondents had parents who were both Mexican-origin, but two interviewees had a non-Hispanic white parent.

Table A. Demographic Characteristics of Respondents

Age	Number	Percentage
18–35	21	24
36–50	26	30
51–65	22	26
65+	17	20

Sex		
Male	42	49
Female	40	51

Education		
Less than high school	9	10
High school or passed GED	29	34
Some college	20	23
College or more	28	33

Generation		
Immigrant	21	24
Second	37	43
Third or more	28	33

Race on Census		
Mexican Americans		
White	28	43
Other race	37	57
Mexican Immigrants		
White	5	24
Other race	16	76
Total: 86 respondents		

→ **NOTE: Please answer BOTH Questions 5 and 6.**

5. **Is this person Spanish/Hispanic/Latino?** *Mark* ☒ *the* **"No"** *box if* **not** *Spanish/Hispanic/Latino.*

   ☐ **No,** not Spanish/Hispanic/Latino   ☐ Yes, Puerto Rican
   ☐ Yes, Mexican, Mexican Am., Chicano   ☐ Yes, Cuban
   ☐ Yes, other Spanish/Hispanic/Latino — *Print group.* ↗

6. **What is this person's race?** *Mark* ☒ **one or more races** *to indicate what this person considers himself/herself to be.*

   ☐ White
   ☐ Black, African Am., or Negro
   ☐ American Indian or Alaska Native — *Print name of enrolled or principal tribe.* ↗

   ☐ Asian Indian   ☐ Japanese   ☐ Native Hawaiian
   ☐ Chinese   ☐ Korean   ☐ Guamanian or Chamorro
   ☐ Filipino   ☐ Vietnamese   ☐ Samoan
   ☐ Other Asian — *Print race.* ↗   ☐ Other Pacific Islander — *Print race.* ↗

   ☐ Some other race — *Print race.* ↗

Figure A. Census 2000 questions for Hispanic origin and race.

I began my interviews by asking about how they filled out their 2000 U.S. Census form (see Figure A). The specific questions on Hispanic origin and race as they appeared in the 2000 census are shown above. The race options for the 2010 census were identical to those of the 2000 Census. However, as discussed in Chapter Six, the 2010 Census included instructions that stated that Hispanic groups are not races.

Interviews averaged 1–1.5 hours. While some were shorter than average, others lasted over 4 hours. Respondents answered detailed questions about multiple aspects of their lives. Topics covered in the interviews included their family and personal migration histories, race and class composition of the neighborhood where they grew up, details about their current place of residence, the racial and class composition of their social networks over the courses of their lives, messages they received from their parents about their heritage, racial preferences in dating and marriage for themselves and for their children, what they hope to pass on to their children, language use and competence, their perceptions and comfort level regarding other racial/ethnic groups, political and community involvement, and experiences with racial classification and discrimination.

The specific questions I asked regarding external classification and discrimination were of key importance to the study and included the following: "If you were walking down the street here in [city name], and someone were to see you, how do you think the person would label you in terms of your racial or ethnic background? Do you think someone would be able to tell from looking at you that you are [Mexican American/Hispanic/Mexican]? Why do you think they would label you that way?" I then followed up by asking about physical features and other external cues that they felt others use to classify them and inquired: "What about after you introduce yourself, does that change people's perception? If so, why do you think so?" I asked about having an accent or lack of one, Spanish or non-Spanish first and last names, and other details. I then continued: "Has anyone ever commented on your racial or ethnic background, or asked you what your racial or ethnic background is? If so, does this happen often? Can you describe a situation where this has happened? How do you handle such situations? Do you feel that you have ever been discriminated against or treated differently because of your racial and ethnic background? If so, please describe the situation and how you handled it. Do you feel that you have ever benefited from your racial or ethnic background? If so, how?" As these were open-ended interviews, the specific wording of the questions varied conversationally, but all respondents answered these basic questions.

As detailed throughout the book, talking about discrimination was challenging for many respondents, and I took great care and exercised sensitivity in dealing with these issues. Respondents generally felt comfortable disclosing very personal details of their lives with me, and I have been vigilant about protecting the secrecy of their identities in writing the manuscript. Protecting anonymity is of particular concern in the smaller border towns, such as Del Rio, where the population is relatively small. This meant sometimes providing less detail on occupations or other personal characteristics that might compromise anonymity. Because of this issue, I opted to include summary data in the table above rather than detailed information about specific respondents and all their individual characteristics.

Notes

Chapter 1

1. All respondents have been assigned pseudonyms to protect their anonymity. In choosing names for interviewees, I attempted to approximate similar first and last names in terms of language (Spanish vs. English) and the use of English nicknames.

2. The term "Anglo" is commonly used in Texas and some other parts of the Southwest to refer to white European Americans (Montejano 1987). The use of "Anglo" in lieu of "white" reflects the ambiguous racial position of Mexican Americans as "legally white" and "socially nonwhite" (Gómez 2007). This history will be discussed at length later in this chapter. Most of my respondents used both "white" and "Anglo" synonymously to refer to European Americans, and I rely on both terms throughout the book.

3. While the book is focused specifically on Mexican Americans, the debates surrounding the racial status of this group are tied to perceptions of Latinos more generally. Therefore, I couch my discussion by referring to the perception and research involving Latinos, using the term to refer to persons of Spanish-speaking origin.

4. The U.S. Census instructs respondents to answer questions on both Hispanic origin and racial identification. In 2010, the instructions further stated: "For this census Hispanic origins are not races."

5. Respondents are further asked to specify their national origin. Options include "Mexican, Mexican Am., or Chicano," "Puerto Rican," "Cuban," and an "other" write-in option.

6. I use the term "public" in referring to respondents' racial identities on the census because my interviewees acknowledge that their racial responses on the form are directed toward a specific audience: the U.S. government. For example, a Mexican immigrant interviewee who self-identified as Mexicana wrote in "Hispanic" for her race, noting, "The form belongs to the U.S. government and here we are Hispanics."

7. Denton and Massey (1989) read Latino racial responses as reflective of

differences in skin color, arguing that "other race" respondents are racially mixed Latinos occupying an intermediate racial position. Tafoya (2004) argues that racial identities in the census indicate "shades of belonging," that "white" Latinos are more assimilated in U.S. society than those who check "other race."

8. Frankenberg uses the phrase "color and power evasive" to discuss the discursive strategies of her white women respondents in articulating racial ideologies that "evade" talking about race and inevitably power.

9. See Foley (1998) and Gómez (2007) for detailed histories of Mexican Americans' public identifications with whiteness as a strategy of resisting racial discrimination in Texas and New Mexico respectively. See also Anzaldúa (1987) for commentary on the contemporary practice among many Mexican Americans of using multiple-identity labels situationally depending upon context.

10. Sue (2013) and Doremus (2001) note how this racial construction elides the historical presence of other Europeans, Asians, and Africans in Mexico, as well as the contemporary indigenous and afro-mestizo communities.

11. I would like to note that the racial politics of LULAC were far more complex during this time period than I have the space to discuss here. Alongside claims to whiteness, the group oscillated between adopting a steadfast assimilationist stance and celebrating *la raza* and their Mexican ethnic heritage. Moreover, these assertions of whiteness were "public" identities, representing a strategy to combat discrimination and not necessarily representative of the personal identities of group members. See Cynthia E. Orozco's (2009) book, *No Mexicans, Women, or Dogs Allowed: The Rise of the Mexican American Civil Rights Movement*, for a more detailed discussion of the history and contributions of LULAC.

12. See Cristina G. Mora's (forthcoming) book, *Making Hispanics: How Activists, Bureaucrats, and Media Constructed a New American*, for a detailed analysis of development of the "Hispanic" category on the 1980 U.S. Census.

13. In 2010, for example, 90% of Latinos selected either "white" alone (53%) or "other race" alone (37%). Six percent chose "more than one race," while the remaining 4% answered black, American Indian, or Asian. Source: U.S. Census 2010 via American FactFinder, accessed January 2013 from http://factfinder2.census.gov/faces/nav/jsf/pages/index.xhtml.

14. Source: U.S. Census 2010 via American FactFinder, accessed January 2013 from http://factfinder2.census.gov/faces/nav/jsf/pages/index.xhtml.

15. Modeling the probability of labeling as "other race" vs. "white" using 2000 Census data in a statewide analysis of Mexican American responses in Texas, I found those who were older, U.S.-born, and who had higher levels of education were more likely to identify as "white." As stated here, those in the lowest income groups were most likely to label themselves as "white." Speaking Spanish in the home increased the odds of labeling as "other race" by only 5% (Dowling 2004).

16. Telles and Ortiz (2008) hypothesize that heightened self-identification as white among Mexican Americans in Texas may be related to a specific regional history of courting whiteness. However, an examination of the meaning of this whiteness was beyond the scope of their study.

17. While not specifically focused on formal racial classification, Carleen Basler (2008) explores how naturalized Mexican immigrants utilize discourses of whiteness in their attitudes toward policies affecting undocumented immigrants.

18. Caribbeans and Central and South Americans make up only 5% and 3% of the Latino population in Dallas and Fort Worth respectively. These groups constitute less than 1% of the Latino population in Del Rio and Mission, and 1.5% of the Latino population in McAllen.

19. Statistics obtained from Census 2010, using American FactFinder for Tarrant and Dallas Counties.

20. Statistics obtained from Census 2010, using American FactFinder for Hidalgo County.

21. Statistics obtained from Census 2010, using American FactFinder for Val Verde County.

22. When I began this project as a graduate student many years ago, I originally planned on a rather ambitious five-site study that included San Antonio and Austin as well. I conducted some exploratory interviews in both these locations, before deciding to focus my book on the three communities of Dallas/Fort Worth, Mission/McAllen, and Del Rio.

23. I conducted all interviews personally, including those in Spanish. However, as a multigenerational Mexican American, I do not have the same competency in Spanish as a native speaker. To assure that there would be no communication barrier, on all but one of those interviews conducted completely in Spanish, I brought a native-speaking assistant with me. Typically, the assistant did not need to offer any help, but her presence allowed me to feel confident that there would be no missed communication. One Spanish interview was conducted without the presence of an assistant. The interviewee was fluent in English, but upon my arrival for the interview said that she would feel more comfortable in Spanish, and so we switched.

Chapter 2

1. O'Brien (2008) also notes how such minimization of race and racism may also be the result of a desensitization that occurs through continuous exposure to discriminatory practices. Essed (1991) refers to this phenomenon as "everyday racism." Essentially, Essed argues that racist encounters can become so much a part of daily life that for many people of color they become unremarkable. I found this phenomenon in some of my respondents' narratives and note this where applicable.

2. This project very clearly centers on the experiences of Mexican Americans and Mexican immigrants, giving voice to marginalized communities and decentering Eurocentric interpretations. Such practices have become the cornerstone of scholarship in Chicano/Latino Studies and Women's Studies, as these disciplines seek to place the narratives of racial and gender minorities at the forefront (Collins 1991; Delgado Bernal 1998).

3. Indeed, across the spectrum of racial ideology, no U.S.-born Mexican Americans ever listed other Mexican Americans as racially different from themselves, regardless of variation in skin color or class background. If they identified themselves as racially white, then they placed all Mexican Americans in this racial category. Moreover, when I asked about how respondents would fill out

the race question for other household members, none identified Mexican American family members as racially different from themselves, even when their spouse/child was comparatively darker or lighter skinned. This provides further evidence that racial responses on the census are not a direct reflection of skin color for Mexican Americans.

Chapter 3

1. The woman who identified as "Chicana" for her race on the census actually did not define the term as a politicized label. Rather, she described a "Chicano/a" as someone who was more assimilated and English-speaking, like herself. She was the only Mexican American to define the term in that way. Primarily Mexican immigrants used this definition of "Chicano/a."

Chapter 4

1. Just as racial labels vary by region and specific context in the United States, the meaning of race and color terminology in Mexico is neither universal nor static. *Raza, güero,* and *moreno* can be used differently dependent upon location, audience, and context. For example, while *raza* is frequently used to refer to peoplehood, it can also be used by upper-class Mexicans to refer to lower-class persons in Mexico; *moreno* is used to describe brown skin color, but it is also used in some contexts as a polite way to refer to persons who are phenotypically black (Doremus 2001; Sue 2013).

2. Recognition of blackness in Mexico varies regionally and has shifted considerably over time (Sue 2013).

3. Forms for the Mexican Census may be viewed on the Instituto Nacional de Estadística Geografía (INEGI) website: http://www.inegi.org.mx/. The form includes no questions regarding "race," but it does contain questions regarding the use of indigenous languages and membership in indigenous communities.

4. See Sue (2013) for an analysis of the disconnect between Mexico's national discourse that denies racial difference and the realities of "race" or color inequalities that persist in contemporary Mexico.

Chapter 5

1. See Mora (forthcoming) for a detailed history of the development of Latino/Hispanic panethicity and its relationship to both political ideology and the state.

2. Valdez (2011) provides additional research demonstrating how panethnic labels can be employed when Latinos distance themselves from other Latino groups. Interviewing Latino entrepreneurs in Houston, Valdez finds that restaurant owners would frequently use "Latino" or "Hispanic" to describe other Lati-

nos who are not co-ethnics. For example, a Salvadoran respondent in the study judges the Salvadoran work ethic as superior to that of "Latinos."

3. This finding parallels Vila's (2000) research in which he notes that Mexican Americans frequently describe "all poverty as Mexican." Even when Mexican Americans in Vila's study were shown images of poverty from their own neighborhoods in El Paso, they still maintained an association that poverty is "Mexican" and not "American." I argue that similarly, Mexican American respondents associate discrimination with "Mexican" identity.

Chapter 6

1. Throughout the book, I have cited three notable exceptions to this interpretation of Latino racial responses: Rodríguez (2000), Roth (2010), and Gómez (2007). In Rodríguez's (2000) east coast–based study of primarily Caribbeans and South Americans, she finds that race for Latinos represents a "social" or "political" concept rather than one that is biologically determined. Wendy Roth (2010) similarly argues that Latino racial labeling on the census does not merely reflect skin color for Puerto Rican and Dominican immigrants in her New York–based study. Rather, she argues that these Latino immigrants struggle with competing definitions of race from both the United States and their respective home countries, often identifying in ways that do not match how they are seen and classified by others. Finally, Gómez (2007) hypothesizes that whiteness on the census may reflect a defensive strategy against racism.

2. In particular, Tafoya does acknowledge that Texas has an exceptionally high percentage of Latinos who identify as "white." Noting possible factors that could be informing this, she writes (2004: 2): "This is the only state where a large Latino population was caught up both in Southern-style racial segregation and then the civil rights struggle to undo it." However, despite her caveat that racial labeling for Latinos may be complex in this regard, she still maintains that Latino racial responses are reflective of "shades of belonging," whereby white Latinos feel more accepted by society than those who indicate "other race."

3. Roth (2010) also corroborates this finding that census racial identification is not a direct reflection of color. Telles and Ortiz (2008) further find that skin color is not significantly linked to racial responses for Mexican Americans in San Antonio, Texas, and Los Angeles, California.

4. As stated in the previous chapter, Ochoa's (2004) work confirms this finding that fluidity in racial labeling among Mexican Americans does not indicate flexibility.

5. To provide a brief anecdotal story on this issue, when I was an instructor at the University of Texas at Austin, Mexican American students in my Chicano/a Studies classes frequently were unaware before taking the class of the realities of segregation and discrimination their parents and grandparents faced. During the course of the semester, many would talk to their parents about what they were learning, only to discover that their parents and/or grandparents went to "Mexican schools," faced corporal punishment for speaking Spanish, were denied access

to recreational facilities in their hometowns, or experienced all these situations. The lack of accurate historical representations of Texas history in high schools in the state likely contributes to this phenomenon. My interviews suggest, however, that a parental desire to protect their children from these harsh realities may also have been a big factor in this.

6. Suzanne Oboler (1995) details these debates regarding terminology and further problematizes "Latino" as also Eurocentric in its emphasis on "Latin" or other European origins.

7. Focus groups from the U.S. Census Bureau's recent Alternative Questionnaire Experiment (AQE) further revealed that many Latinos felt that these instructions on the 2010 Census discouraged them from writing in Latino identifiers under the "other race" option (Compton et al. 2012).

8. For more detail regarding the AQE methods and findings, see the full report published by the U.S. Census Bureau: Compton et al. (2012), "2010 Census Race and Hispanic Origin Alternative Questionnaire Experiment: Final Report."

9. A total of 488,604 households received the alternative questionnaires. The overall mail return rate ranges from 78.2% to 80.5% (Compton et al. 2012).

10. This component of the study included 67 focus groups, for a total of 768 participants. Focus groups were conducted in 26 U.S. cities and included a number of population groups: whites, blacks, Latinos, American Indians, Asians, multiracials, and Afro-Caribbeans, among others (Compton et al. 2012).

11. Four of the questionnaire designs listed "Latino/Hispanic origin" (or specific Latino national-origin groups) alongside racial groups in a combined-question format.

12. See Ennis et al. (2011) for the racial breakdown of Latinos in the 2010 Census. The percentage of Latinos who identified as "white" in the AQE is drawn from the March 2013 U.S. Census Bureau memorandum: "2010 Census Race and Hispanic Origin Alternative Questionnaire Experiment Supplemental Analysis: Race Distributions by Hispanic Origin" (U.S. Census Bureau DSSD Decennial Census Memorandum Series #0-B-14-R1).

13. Specific racial tabulations from Latino AQE respondents are available in the March 2013 supplemental analysis memorandum cited above.

14. Of the four combined formats, I personally believe the "streamlined" and "very streamlined" designs represent the best options. Both these versions allow all groups, including whites and blacks, to further write in detailed information about their origin. In the "streamlined" option (Figure 6.1), the write-in boxes for origins are provided after each category. In the "very streamlined" format, the boxes to elaborate on one's specific origin are instead provided in a subsequent question directly following the question on "race or origin." These and all tested questionnaire formats can be viewed in the full AQE report (Compton et al. 2012).

15. The Census Bureau's AQE survey also found that African Americans felt the term "Negro" was outdated and offensive and should be eliminated from their category so that it reads "Black or African American." I concur with this suggestion.

References

Alba, Richard. 2006. "Mexican Americans and the American Dream." *Perspectives on Politics* 4: 289–296.

Alcoff, Linda Martín. 2000. "Is Latina/o Identity a Racial Identity?" In Jorge J. E. Gracia and Pablo De Greiff (eds.), *Hispanics/Latinos in the United States: Ethnicity, Race, and Rights*, 23–44. New York: Routledge.

Almaguer, Tomás. 1994. *Racial Faultlines: The Historical Origins of White Supremacy in California*. Berkeley: University of California Press.

Anderson, Margo J. 1988. *The American Census: A Social History*. New Haven, CT: Yale University Press.

Anzaldúa, Gloria. 1987. *Borderlands/La Frontera*. San Francisco, CA: Aunt Lute Books.

Arellano, Gustavo. 2010. "Ask a Mexican: Special Census Edition." Accessed January 2013 from http://www.riverfronttimes.com/2010-04-07/news/ask-a-mexican-special-census-edition/.

Bailey, Stanley R. 2009. *Legacies of Race: Identities, Attitudes, and Politics in Brazil*. Stanford, CA: Stanford University Press.

Basler, Carleen. 2008. "White Dreams and Red Votes: Mexican Americans and the Lure of Inclusion in the Republican Party." *Ethnic and Racial Studies* 31(1): 123–166.

Bonilla-Silva, Eduardo. 2001. *White Supremacy and Racism in the Post-Civil Rights Era*. Boulder, CO: Lynne Rienner.

———. 2004. "From Bi-racial to Tri-racial: Towards a New System of Racial Identification in the USA." *Ethnic and Racial Studies* 27(6): 931–950.

———. 2010. *Racism without Racists: Color-blind Racism and the Persistence of Racial Inequality in the United States*. Lanham, MD: Rowman & Littlefield Publishers.

Bonilla-Silva, Eduardo, Tyrone A. Foreman, Amanda E. Lewis, and David G. Embrick. 2003. "'It Wasn't Me!' How Will Race and Racism Work in 21st Century America." *Research in Political Sociology* 12: 111–134.

Buchanan, Patrick J. 2007. *State of Emergency: The Third World Invasion and Conquest of America*. New York: St Martin's Press.

Camarillo, Albert M. 1971. "Research Note on Chicano Community Leaders: The G.I. Generation." *Aztlán* 2(1): 145–150.

Chapa, Jorge. 2000. "Hispanic Population." In Margo J. Anderson (ed.), *Encyclopedia of the U.S. Census*, 241–246. Washington, DC: CQ Press.

Chavez, Leo R. 2008. *The Latino Threat: Constructing Immigrants, Citizens, and the Nation*. Stanford, CA: Stanford University Press.

Citrin, Jack, Amy Lerman, Michael Marakami, and Kathryn Pearson. 2007. "Testing Huntington: Is Hispanic Immigration a Threat to American Identity?" *Perspectives on Politics* 5(1): 31–48.

Collins, Patricia Hill. 1991. *Black Feminist Thought: Knowledge, Consciousness, and the Politics of Empowerment*. New York: Routledge.

Compton, Elizabeth, Michael Bentley, Sharon Ennis, and Sonya Rastogi. 2012. "2010 Census Race and Hispanic Origin Alternative Questionnaire Experiment: Final Report." U.S. Census Bureau, Washington, DC.

Cornell, Stephen, and Douglas Hartmann. 1997. *Ethnicity and Race: Making Identities in a Changing World*. Thousand Oaks, CA: Pine Forge Press.

Davis, F. James. 1991. *Who Is Black? One Nation's Definition*. University Park: The Pennsylvania State University Press.

De Genova, Nicholas, and Ana Y. Ramos-Zayas. 2003. *Latino Crossings: Mexicans, Puerto Ricans, and the Politics of Race and Citizenship*. New York: Routledge.

Deans-Smith, Susan, and Ilona Katzew. 2009. "Introduction: The Alchemy of Race in Mexican America." In Ilona Katzew and Susan Deans-Smith (eds.), *Race and Classification: The Case of Mexican America*, 1–24. Stanford, CA: Stanford University Press.

Delgado Bernal, Dolores. 1998. "Using Chicana Feminist Epistemology in Educational Research." *Harvard Educational Review* 68(4): 552–582.

Denton, Nancy A., and Douglas S. Massey. 1989. "Racial Identity Among Caribbean Hispanics: The Effect of Double Minority Status on Residential Segregation." *American Sociological Review* 54: 790–808.

Doremus, Anne. 2001. "Indigenism, Mestizaje, and National Identity in Mexico during the 1940s and the 1950s." *Mexican Studies/Estudios Mexicanos* 17(2): 375–402.

Dowling, Julie A. 2004. "The Lure of Whiteness and the Politics of Otherness: Mexican American Racial Identity." Doctoral dissertation: The University of Texas at Austin.

———. 2005. "'I'm Not Mexican . . . Pero Soy Mexicano': Linguistic Context of Labeling Among Mexican Americans in Texas." *Southwest Journal of Linguistics* 1: 53–63.

Dowling, Julie A., and C. Alison Newby. 2010. "So Far from Miami: Afro-Cuban Encounters with Mexicans in the U.S. Southwest." *Latino Studies* 8(2): 176–194.

Ennis, Sharon R., Merarys Ríos-Vargas, and Nora G. Albert. 2011. *The Hispanic Population: 2010*. Washington, DC: U.S. Census Bureau Report C2010BR-04, May 2011.

Espiritu, Yen Le. 1992. *Asian American Panethnicity: Bridging Institutions and Identities*. Philadelphia, PA: Temple University Press.

Essed, Philomena. 1991. *Understanding Everyday Racism: An Interdisciplinary Theory.* Newbury Park, CA: Sage Publications.

Feagin, Joe R. 2010. *The White Racial Frame: Centuries of Racial Framing and Counter-Framing.* New York: Routledge.

Feagin, Joe R., and José A. Cobas. 2008. "Latinos/as and White Racial Frame: The Procrustean Bed of Assimilation." *Sociological Inquiry* 78(1): 39–53.

Foley, Neil. 1997. *The White Scourge: Mexicans, Blacks, and Poor Whites in Texas Cotton Culture.* Berkeley: University of California Press.

———. 1998. "Becoming Hispanic: Mexican Americans and the Faustian Pact with Whiteness." In Neil Foley (ed.), *Reflexiones 1997: New Directions in Mexican American Studies,* 53–70. Austin, TX: Center for Mexican American Studies.

———. 2006. "Over the Rainbow: *Hernandez v. Texas, Brown v. Board of Education,* and *Black v. Brown.*" In Michael A. Olivas (ed.), *"Colored Men" and "Hombres Aquí": Hernandez v. Texas and the Emergence of Mexican-American Lawyering,* 111–121. Houston, TX: Arte Público Press.

Frank, Reanne, Ilana Redstone Akresh, and Bo Lu. 2010. "Latino Immigrants and the U.S. Racial Order: How and Where Do They Fit in?" *American Sociological Review* 73(3): 378–401.

Frankenberg, Ruth. 1993. *White Women, Race Matters: The Social Construction of Whiteness.* Minneapolis: University of Minnesota Press.

Gallagher, Charles A. 2003. "Color-blind Privilege: The Social and Political Functions of Erasing the Color Line in Post Race America." *Race, Gender and Class* 10(4): 22–37.

García, John A. 1996. "The Chicano Movement: Its Legacy for Politics and Policy." In David R. Maciel and Isidro D. Ortiz (eds.), *Chicanas/Chicanos at the Crossroads: Social, Economic, and Political Change,* 83–107. Tucson: University of Arizona Press.

García, Mario T. 1989. *Mexican Americans: Leadership, Ideology, and Identity, 1930–1960.* New Haven, CT: Yale University Press.

García Bedolla, Lisa. 2005. *Fluid Borders: Latino Power, Identity, and Politics in Los Angeles.* Berkeley: University of California Press.

Golash-Boza, Tanya. 2006. "Dropping the Hyphen? Becoming Latino(a)-American through Racialized Assimilation." *Social Forces* 85(1): 27–54.

Golash-Boza, Tanya, and William Darity Jr. 2008. "Latino Racial Choices: The Effects of Skin Colour and Discrimination on Latinos' and Latinas' Racial Self-Identifications." *Ethnic and Racial Studies* 31(5): 899–934.

Goldsmith, Pat Rubio, Mary Romero, Raquel Rubio-Goldsmith, Manuel Escobedo, and Laura Khoury. 2009. "Ethno-Racial Profiling and State Violence in a Southwest Barrio." *Aztlán: A Journal of Chicano Studies* 34(1): 93–123.

Gómez, Laura E. 2007. *Manifest Destinies: The Making of the Mexican American Race.* New York: New York University Press.

Gordon, Milton M. 1964. *Assimilation in American Life: The Role of Race, Religion, and National Origins.* New York: Oxford University Press.

Gross, Ariela J. 2003. "Texas Mexicans and the Politics of Whiteness." *Law and History Review* 21(1): 195–205.

Gutiérrez, David G. 1995. *Walls and Mirrors: Mexican Americans, Mexican Immigrants, and the Politics of Ethnicity.* Berkeley: University of California Press.

Gutiérrez, Ramón A. 2009. "Hispanic Identities in the Southwestern United States." In Ilona Katzew and Susan Deans-Smith (eds.), *Race and Classification: The Case of Mexican America*, 174–193. Stanford, CA: Stanford University Press.

Hale, Grace Elizabeth. 1998. *Making Whiteness: The Culture of Segregation in the South, 1890–1940*. New York: Vintage.

Haney-Lopez, Ian F. 1996. *White by Law: The Legal Construction of Race*. New York: New York University Press.

Harris, Cheryl I. 1993. "Whiteness as Property." *Harvard Law Review* 106: 1709–1791.

Huntington, Samuel P. 2004. *Who Are We? The Challenges to America's National Identity*. New York: Simon & Schuster.

Hurtado, Aida, Patricia Gurin, and Timothy Peng. 1994. "Social Identities—A Framework for Studying the Adaptations of Immigrants and Ethnics: The Adaptations of Mexicans in the United States." *Social Problems* 41: 129–150.

Ignatiev, Noel. 1995. *How the Irish Became White*. New York: Routledge.

Inda, Jonathan Xavier. 2006. *Targeting Immigrants: Government, Technology, and Ethics*. Malden, MA: Blackwell Publishing.

Itzigsohn, José. 2004. "The Formation of Latino and Latina Panethnic Identities." In Nancy Foner and George M. Fredrickson (eds.), *Not Just Black and White: Historical and Contemporary Perspectives on Immigration, Race, and Ethnicity in the United States*, 197–216. New York: Russell Sage Foundation.

Jenkins, Richard. 1997. *Rethinking Ethnicity: Arguments and Explorations*. New York: Russell Sage Foundation.

Jiménez, Tomás R. 2010. *Replenished Ethnicity: Mexican Americans, Immigration, and Identity*. Berkeley: University of California Press.

Jones-Correa, Michael A. 1998. *Between Two Nations: The Political Predicament of Latinos in New York City*. Ithaca, NY: Cornell University Press.

Jones-Correa, Michael A., and David L. Leal. 1996. "Becoming 'Hispanic': Secondary Pan-Ethnic Identification Among Latin American–Origin Populations in the United States." *Hispanic Journal of Behavioral Sciences* 18: 214–255.

Lee, Jennifer, and Frank D. Bean. 2004. "America's Changing Color Lines: Immigration, Race/Ethnicity, and Multiracial Identification." *Annual Review of Sociology* 30: 221–242.

Lee, Sharon M. 1993. "Racial Classifications in the U.S. Census: 1890–1990." *Ethnic and Racial Studies* 16: 75–94.

Lerner, Victoria. 1979. *La Educación Socialista*. Mexico City: El Colegio de Mexico.

Lipsitz, George. 1998. *The Possessive Investment in Whiteness: How White People Profit from Identity Politics*. Philadelphia, PA: Temple University Press.

Macias, Thomas. 2006. *Mestizo in America: Generations of Mexican Ethnicity in the Suburban Southwest*. Tucson: University of Arizona Press.

Marquez, Benjamin. 2003. *Constructing Identities in Mexican-American Political Organizations: Choosing Issues, Taking Sides*. Austin: University of Texas Press.

Menchaca, Martha. 2001. *Recovering History, Constructing Race: The Indian, Black, and White Roots of Mexican Americans*. Austin: University of Texas Press.

Mindiola, Tatcho, Jr., Yolanda Flores Niemann, and Nestor Rodriguez. 2002. *Black-Brown Relations and Stereotypes*. Austin: University of Texas Press.

Montejano, David. 1987. *Anglos and Mexicans in the Making of Texas, 1836–1986*. Austin: University of Texas Press.

Mora, G. Cristina. Forthcoming. *Making Hispanics: How Activists, Bureaucrats, and Media Constructed a New American*. Chicago: University of Chicago Press.

Morrison, Toni. 1993. "On the Backs of Blacks." *Time*, December 2: 57.

Murguía, Edward. 1975. *Assimilation, Colonialism and the Mexican American People*. Austin, TX: Center for Mexican American Studies.

Murguía, Edward, and Edward E. Telles. 1996. "Phenotype and Schooling Among Mexican Americans." *Sociology of Education* 69: 276–289.

Murguía, Edward, and Tyrone Foreman. 2003. "Shades of Whiteness: The Mexican American Experience in Relation to Anglos and Blacks." In Ashley M. Doane and Eduardo Bonilla-Silva (eds.), *White Out: The Continuing Significance of Racism*. New York: Routledge.

Nagel, Joane. 1994. "Constructing Ethnicity: Creating and Recreating Ethnic Identity and Culture." *Social Problems* 41: 152–176.

Nevins, Joseph. 2010. *Operation Gatekeeper and Beyond: The War on "Illegals" and the Remaking of the U.S.-Mexico Boundary*. New York: Routledge.

Newby, C. Alison, and Julie A. Dowling. 2007. "Black and Hispanic: The Racial Identification of Afro-Cuban Immigrants in the Southwest." *Sociological Perspectives* 50(3): 343–366.

Nieto-Phillips, John M. 2004. *The Language of Blood: The Making of Spanish-American Identity in New Mexico, 1880s–1930s*. Albuquerque: University of New Mexico Press.

Nobles, Melissa. 2000. *Shades of Citizenship: Race and Census in Modern Politics*. Stanford, CA: Stanford University Press.

Oboler, Suzanne. 1995. *Ethnic Labels, Latino Lives: Identity and the Politics of (Re) Presentation in the United States*. Minneapolis: University of Minnesota Press.

O'Brien, Eileen. 2008. *The Racial Middle: Latinos and Asian Americans Living Beyond the Racial Divide*. New York: New York University Press.

Ochoa, Gilda. 2004. *Becoming Neighbors in a Mexican American Community: Power, Conflict, and Solidarity*. Austin: University of Texas Press.

Omi, Michael, and Howard Winant. 1994. *Racial Formation in the United States*. New York: Routledge.

Orozco, Cynthia E. 2009. *No Mexicans, Women, or Dogs Allowed: The Rise of the Mexican American Civil Rights Movement*. Austin: University of Texas Press.

Padilla, Felix M. 1984. "On the Nature of Latino Ethnicity." *Social Science Quarterly* 65: 651–664.

———. 1985. *Latino Ethnic Consciousness: The Case of Mexican Americans and Puerto Ricans in Chicago*. Notre Dame, IN: University of Notre Dame Press.

Park, Robert Ezra. 1950. *Race and Culture*. Glencoe, IL: Free Press.

Pascoe, Peggy. 1991. "Race, Gender, and Intercultural Relations: The Case of Interracial Marriage." *Frontiers: A Journal of Women's Studies* 12(1): 5–18.

Patterson, Orlando. 2001. "Race by the Numbers." *New York Times*, May 8: A27.

Richardson, Chad. 1999. *Batos, Bolillos, Pochos, and Pelados: Class and Culture on the South Texas Border*. Austin: University of Texas Press.

Rodríguez, Clara E. 1992. "Race, Culture, and Latino 'Otherness' in the 1980 Census." *Social Science Quarterly* 73: 930–937.

———. 2000. *Changing Race: Latinos, the Census, and the History of Ethnicity in the United States.* New York: New York University Press.

Roediger, David R. 1991. *The Wages of Whiteness: Race and the Making of the American Working Class.* New York: Verso.

———. 2002. *Colored White: Transcending the Racial Past.* Berkeley: University of California Press.

Roth, Wendy D. 2010. "Racial Mismatch: The Divergence between Form and Function in Data for Monitoring Racial Discrimination of Hispanics." *Social Science Quarterly* 91(5): 1288–1311.

———. 2012. *Race Migrations: Latinos and the Cultural Transformation of Race.* Stanford, CA: Stanford University Press.

Sheridan, Clare. 2003. "'Another White Race': Mexican Americans and the Paradox of Whiteness in Jury Selection." *Law and Historical Review* 21(2003): 109.

Sue, Christina A. 2013. *Land of the Cosmic Race: Race Mixture, Racism, and Blackness in Mexico.* New York: Oxford University Press.

Tafoya, Sonya. 2004. "Shades of Belonging." Washington, DC: Pew Hispanic Center, December 6. Accessed January 2013 from http://www.pewhispanic.org/2004/12/06/shades-of-belonging/.

Takaki, Ronald. 1993. *A Different Mirror: A History of Multicultural America.* Boston, MA: Little, Brown and Company.

Taylor, William B. 2009. "Preface." In Ilona Katzew and Susan Deans-Smith (eds.), *Race and Classification: The Case of Mexican America*, ix–xviii. Stanford, CA: Stanford University Press.

Telles, Edward E., and Edward Murguía. 1990. "Phenotypic Discrimination and Income Differences Among Mexican Americans." *Social Science Quarterly* 71: 682–696.

Telles, Edward E., and Vilma Ortiz. 2008. *Generations of Exclusion: Mexican Americans, Assimilation, and Race.* New York: Russell Sage Foundation.

Tienda, Marta, and Faith Mitchell. 2006. *Multiple Origins, Uncertain Destinies: Hispanics and the American Future.* Washington, DC: National Academies Press.

Tuan, Mia. 1998. *Forever Foreigners or Honorary Whites? The Asian Ethnic Experience Today.* New Brunswick, NJ: Rutgers University Press.

U.S. Census Bureau. 1997. "Results of the 1996 Racial and Ethnic Targeted Test." Population Division Working Paper No. 18. U.S. Census Bureau, Washington, DC.

U.S. Census Bureau. 2013. "2010 Census Race and Hispanic Origin Alternative Questionnaire Experiment Supplemental Analysis: Race Distributions by Hispanic Origin." U.S. Census Bureau DSSD Decennial Census Memorandum Series #0-B-14-R1.

Valdez, Zulema. 2011. *The New Entrepreneurs: How Race, Class, and Gender Shape American Enterprise.* Stanford, CA: Stanford University Press.

Vasquez, Jessica M. 2011. *Mexican Americans Across Generations: Immigrant Families, Racial Realities.* New York: New York University Press.

Vila, Pablo. 2000. *Crossing Borders, Reinforcing Borders: Social Categories, Metaphors, and Narrative Identities on the U.S.-Mexico Frontier*. Austin: University of Texas Press.

———. 2003. "The Polysemy of the Label 'Mexican' on the Border." In Pablo Vila (ed.), *Ethnography at the Border*, 105–140. Minneapolis: University of Minnesota Press.

Viruell-Fuentes, Edna A. 2007. "Beyond Acculturation: Immigration, Discrimination, and Health Research Among Mexicans in the United States." *Social Science and Medicine* 65: 1524–1535.

Waters, Mary C. 1990. *Ethnic Options: Choosing Identities in America*. Berkeley: University of California Press.

Yancey, George. 2003. *Who Is White? Latinos, Asians, and the New Black/Nonblack Divide*. Boulder, CO: Lynne Rienner.

Index

U.S. categories for, 21, 79, 81, 82–83; white Americans' denial of, 24. *See also* racial identification; racial ideology; racial "otherness"; racial profiling; racism; segregation

racial identification: citizenship as factor in, 16; dialogue between external and internal identities in making, 8, 9–10, 62–63; discrimination in, 76; in everyday interactions, 21, 35, 41, 87, 90; and identities assigned in relation to whiteness, 9; by immigrants, 21, 84–88, 96; of Latinos, 3–9; Latinos and whiteness in, 4–5; negotiation of, by Mexican immigrants in the U.S. context, 82–84; migration and, 96–97; and negotiating racial labeling in daily life, 98–115; and U.S. Census in construction of racial identities, 12; as white by Mexican Americans in the U.S. Census, 1, 2, 3, 5–7, 11–12, 14–15, 20, 25, 27, 29, 33–36, 39, 40, 41, 44, 45, 47, 48, 49–50, 75–76, 87, 88, 118, 122–125, 133–134, 140n15. *See also* racial "otherness"

racial ideology: continuum, 6, 20, 25, 26, 65, 118–120; disconnection between public and private articulations of race and role of, 3, 8, 118; everyday racial identification influenced by, 21; factors that influence, 27, 122; as influencing process of identity assertion, 8; racial labeling linked to, 103, 114, 120, 121, 133; shifts in, 25. *See also* anti-racist ideology; color-blind racial ideology

racial "otherness": discrimination in, 21; factors in, 52; helping children embrace, 66; and Latinos who formally identify as other, 96; Mexican Americans choosing between whiteness and, 5–8, 16; and resistance to racial "othering" by Mexican Americans, 7

racial profiling: of Mexican Ameri-

cans, 7, 44, 50, 63–64, 68, 69, 119; minimizing, 54

racism: in color-blind racial ideology, 32; cultural, 24, 30–31, 94; everyday, 47, 56, 141n1; as fundamental component of whiteness, 23; as institutional, 75; and "leaving racism in the past" view, 26, 27, 38–44, 46; Mexican American probation officer accused of, 61–62; against Mexican Americans, 33, 38, 44, 56, 63, 65, 66, 68, 73, 128; Mexican identity asserted when confronted with, 107; Mexican immigrants experience, 84; "Mexican" label and countering, 121; minimization of, 15, 24, 25, 27, 33, 40, 44, 47, 49, 53, 54, 56, 60, 61, 63, 65, 68, 75, 76, 77, 106, 124, 141n1; naturalization of, 24, 47, 49, 56, 63, 66–67; as phase on way to acceptance as American, 48; and "race/racism is transient" view, 26, 27, 44–49, 67; and "racism is endemic" view, 26, 53, 68–75; and "racism is minimal" view, 26, 53, 54–63; and "racism is significant" view, 26, 53, 63–68; talking about, seen as un-American, 76. *See also* anti-racist ideology

Ramos-Zayas, Ana Y., 99
Raza Unida, La, 11, 39, 48, 67, 74
Reyes, Tom, 47–48
Rivera, Manuel "Meme," 51, 52, 55, 58
Rodríguez, Clara E., 13, 14, 20, 51–52, 96, 116, 128, 143n1
Rodríguez, Frank, 48–49
Roediger, David, 133
Roth, Wendy D., 13–14, 85, 96, 143n1, 143n3
Ruiz, Marisol, 92–95, 96, 114

Salinas, Joe, 41
Sanchez, Juliana, 2–3, 4, 6, 72–73, 107
Sandoval, Tomás, 108–109

117; as best way to be seen as American, 104; citizenship tied to, 92; emergence of, 23; European American construction of, 117; European Americans' investment in, 133; meaning of, for Mexican Americans, 23–50; Mexican Americans choosing between racial "otherness" and, 5–8, 16; Mexican Americans combatting discrimination with claims of, 10–11, 50, 74, 119; Mexican Americans identifying outside bounds of, 51–77; Mexican Americans' strategic use of, 2, 6, 11–12, 22, 29–30, 32, 39, 50, 123, 133; as property, 133; as "raceless" category, 36, 118; racial identities assigned in relation to, 9; as racial frame, 8, 20, 23–25, 52. *See also* white identity; whites

whites: as Anglos, 139n2; assertions of Mexicanness by Mexican Americans who self-identify as, 106–107; assimilation versus being accepted as, 66; in Dallas/Fort Worth (DFW) Metroplex, 17; in Del Rio, 18; immigrants who identify as, on census, 83, 84, 87–92, 96; Latinos becoming racially white, 4–5; Latinos who self-label as, 13, 14, 96, 116–117, 130, 132, 140n13; *mestizaje* and whitening, 93; Mexican Americans legally constructed as, 10, 48, 76; Mexican Americans who identify on census as, 1, 2, 3, 5–7, 11–12, 14–15, 20, 25, 27, 29, 33–36, 39, 40, 41, 44, 45, 47, 48, 49–50, 75–76, 87, 88, 118, 122–125, 133–134, 140n15; Mexican Americans who see themselves as, 29, 37, 141n3; in Mission/McAllen, 18; status of, in Mexico, 80; in U.S. racial system, 79. *See also* European Americans; white identity; whiteness

work ethic, 24, 30, 36, 37

Yancey, George, 4, 5, 6, 117

CPSIA information can be obtained
at www.ICGtesting.com
Printed in the USA
FSOW01n1331190116
15835FS

9 781477 307540